Cambridge Elements

Elements in Language, Gender and Sexuality
edited by
Helen Sauntson
York St John University

LANGUAGE, GENDER AND BIOPOLITICS

Meaning-Making and Intersex Variations in Healthcare

Brian W. King
The University of Hong Kong

Shaftesbury Road, Cambridge CB2 8EA, United Kingdom

One Liberty Plaza, 20th Floor, New York, NY 10006, USA

477 Williamstown Road, Port Melbourne, VIC 3207, Australia

314–321, 3rd Floor, Plot 3, Splendor Forum, Jasola District Centre, New Delhi – 110025, India

103 Penang Road, #05–06/07, Visioncrest Commercial, Singapore 238467

Cambridge University Press is part of Cambridge University Press & Assessment, a department of the University of Cambridge.

We share the University's mission to contribute to society through the pursuit of education, learning and research at the highest international levels of excellence.

www.cambridge.org
Information on this title: www.cambridge.org/9781009532778

DOI: 10.1017/9781009202503

© Brian W. King 2026

This publication is in copyright. Subject to statutory exception and to the provisions of relevant collective licensing agreements, no reproduction of any part may take place without the written permission of Cambridge University Press & Assessment.

When citing this work, please include a reference to the DOI 10.1017/9781009202503

First published 2026

A catalogue record for this publication is available from the British Library

ISBN 978-1-009-53277-8 Hardback
ISBN 978-1-009-20249-7 Paperback
ISSN 2634-8772 (online)
ISSN 2634-8764 (print)

Cambridge University Press & Assessment has no responsibility for the persistence or accuracy of URLs for external or third-party internet websites referred to in this publication and does not guarantee that any content on such websites is, or will remain, accurate or appropriate.

For EU product safety concerns, contact us at Calle de José Abascal, 56, 1°, 28003 Madrid, Spain, or email eugpsr@cambridge.org

Language, Gender and Biopolitics

Meaning-Making and Intersex Variations in Healthcare

Elements in Language, Gender and Sexuality

DOI: 10.1017/9781009202503
First published online: January 2026

Brian W. King
The University of Hong Kong
Author for correspondence: Brian W. King, bwking@hku.hk

Abstract: This Element examines language, power and intersex variations within clinician accounts in Hong Kong, examining how they communicate about intersex traits to patients and their families. Employing interactional sociolinguistics, the research analyses clinician interviews as dynamic social interactions, focusing on how communicative stances are negotiated and social practices are enacted. The Element probes the influence of biopower on clinicians' stances (encompassing gender, sexual difference, racialization and ableism) and explores the possibilities of emancipation from these biopolitical constraints. Findings highlight the tension between medical structuring forces and the formation of intersex subjects and bodies, impacting their autonomy and livability. Gender is relevant as both a power system and a lived reality, critical for understanding the bioregulation of innate sex characteristics and advancing broader implications for gender and language studies and healthcare communication. This research challenges gender-sceptical discourses and highlights the transformative potential of gender frameworks in medical and social contexts.

Keywords: biopower, intersex variations, interactional sociolinguistics, multidimensional gender, stancetaking

© Brian W. King 2026
ISBNs: 9781009532778 (HB), 9781009202497 (PB), 9781009202503 (OC)
ISSNs: 2634-8772 (online), 2634-8764 (print)

Contents

1	Introduction	1
2	Intersex History and Lived Experience	7
3	Biopolitics and Gender in Sociolinguistics	12
4	Research Context, Design and Method	21
5	Crafting Bodies: Biopower, Gender and Intersex Variations	29
6	Crafting Subjects: Biopower, Gender and the Good Parent	44
7	Conclusion	61
	References	67

1 Introduction

The physical sex traits we are born with (i.e., the body parts linked to sex) naturally vary from person to person, existing along a broad spectrum. For most people, these traits are seen as matching fairly well with what society recognizes as binary, either 'male' or 'female'. Some bodies closely align with these cultural ideas, while others are less prototypical but still categorized as one or the other. However, some people's sex traits fall somewhere in the middle of this range, and they are often subjected to medical procedures. How these variations are identified and medically managed (often referred to as *intersex traits* or *differences/disorders of sex development* (Carpenter, 2024; Monro et al., 2025)) involves complex power relationships between doctors, patients and families. Following recent conventions in intersex studies (Balocchi and Kehrer, 2020; Carpenter, 2022; Crocetti et al., 2024; Monro et al., 2025), I will use the term *intersex variations*.

Decisions about whether to perform surgery on people with intersex variations are often made without fully informed consent from the person affected or their guardian (Roen, 2023). In many cases, patients, families and even medical professionals do not fully understand the long-term effects of these procedures (Liao, 2022; Liao and Baratz, 2023). This complex web of power dynamics is closely tied to communication within healthcare, where everyday conversations and institutional systems both shape how meanings and decisions take form.

In this Element, I focus on language, power and intersex variations in accounts of the domain of clinical encounters. I analyse interview accounts by Hong Kong clinicians of how they describe and explain these body traits to parents and patients. It is conducted in the interactional sociolinguistics tradition of discourse analysis (Gumperz, 2015), approaching interviews as joint social interactions and orienting to how social practices are accomplished and stances are negotiated in the here-and-now. It entails examining the interpretation of communicative intent in situ, and analysis is not limited to overtly lexicalized information (i.e., what the words denote). Instead, interactional sociolinguistic analysis examines meaning-making processes closely to ask what the most likely interpretations by interlocutors might be and how they are achieved via assumption and inference (Gumperz, 1999). I use this type of analysis to meet the research aims in this study by examining clinician stance-taking in their accounts of practice to ask:

(1) What stances are animated and elaborated in stancetaking processes about innate sex characteristics, patients and their families in clinician accounts?

(2) Do these stances show evidence of being influenced by the relations of biopower linking gender, sexual difference, racialization and ableism as regulatory structures? If so, what is that evidence?
(3) In what ways are intersex variations and affected subjects unbound from those biopolitics, showing the emancipatory side of gendering?
(4) What do these stances reveal about institutional and personal ideologies concerning the viability and livability of intersex subjects and bodies?

In other words, I probe how those accounts, via the ideologies they reveal through stancetaking, provide clues to both the shaping of subjects and the shaping of innate sex characteristics themselves.

In the analysis, I dissect the articulation and elaboration of stances on intersex variations in the interview accounts of clinicians in Hong Kong. It is a contribution that represents new knowledge and stands to stimulate further knowledge creation in two main ways. Firstly, it does so by localising the Hong Kong context, thereby confronting the colonial and geopolitical hegemonies of Western perspectives on conceptions of intersex embodiment (Rubin, 2017). Secondly, by focusing on biopolitics it permits a re-emphasis of gender as relevant and transformative and enables examination of the meeting place between macro (structure) and micro (agency).

Yet knowledge creation processes are unequal; consequently, people with intersex variations have regularly been the focus of great interest but far less regularly enjoyed meaningful involvement in academic (indeed any) meaning-making about their bodies and lives (Monro et al., 2025). So, it is important to critically self-examine my influence on the research and its influence on me.

I am endosex (i.e., not intersex), a gay man, racialized white and living without disabilities. As an endosex researcher, I have not lived the experience of having my innate sex characteristics acted upon as a 'problem'. As a gay man I have had my own lived experiences of liminality, shame and secrecy, but although fanning the flames of my empathy, these knowledges only negligibly overlap with the lived experience of having intersex variations. Yet, I have conducted projects of social research on the topic of intersex variations over the past fifteen years in New Zealand, the US and Hong Kong. Mindful of my lack of intimate insight into intersex variation, I have closely collaborated with people who do have that insight, working together to generate the research ideas in the first place, to discuss my analyses and to theorize together about analysis and implications (King, 2022a). The present research project is no exception. In terms of conducting this research in Hong Kong, I am a descendant of settler colonists in Canada and New Zealand who has lived and worked in Asia for almost two decades in total, with thirteen years in

Hong Kong teaching local university students in English. This lived experience of Hong Kong society has not provided me with *insider* knowledge of Hong Kong's political economy or sociocultural landscape. It is for these reasons that interactional sociolinguistic analysis is a useful approach to take because it allows me to view meaning-making in action, tempering my preconceptions about the Hong Kong clinicians' intent by attending to what they *convey* about intent and the potential *effects* of what these clinicians reveal in their accounts.

After many discussions with Dr Small Luk, an intersex collaborator in Hong Kong, the idea was hatched to apply for research funding to examine how intersex variations of innate sex characteristics, and the people who live them and their families, are talked about in Hong Kong's plurilingual setting.[1] Luk, a doctor of Chinese medicine and an intersex-identified person and activist, had been acutely aware of terminology and descriptions circulating into Hong Kong in English and Mandarin and being reinterpreted across the clinic and community (King, 2023b). Dr Luk and I agreed that the talk of clinicians who work directly with people with innate sex characteristics should be the primary focus of analysis to find out how they might be traversing this complex linguistic and discursive domain.

I apply the meticulous tools of interactional sociolinguistics to apprehend meaning-making more fully while closely dissecting clinician talk about intersex variations and about the people with whom they are discussed. This linguistic focus complements important qualitative analyses in the US context in which transcripts of clinician-parent interactions were coded to map the course of decision-making about gender assignment (Timmermans et al., 2019) as well as studies in the US (Davis, 2015), UK (Roen and Hegarty, 2018) and Italy (Prandelli and Testoni, 2021) coding for themes in interviews about case management with clinicians and interviews with parents about gender assignment decision-making experiences (Crocetti and Prandelli, 2024). Interactional sociolinguistics brings nuanced insights into the mechanics of meaning-making during social practices as individuals interact and negotiate perceived social norms (Gumperz, 1999, 2015). Focusing more closely on how norms are navigated during interaction (interviews in this case) permits the mechanics of how communication actually works moment to moment to come clearly into view and avoids the 'washing out' of context and meaning-making that necessarily happens when coding is pitched at a very general level to gain an overview of 'higher-level' communication patterns replicable across research contexts (Stubbe et al.,

---

[1] Ethics approval was granted by the Human Research Ethics Committee (HREC) of The University of Hong Kong (HREC Reference Number EA1902017).

2021). Examples of 'higher level' codes would be *direct requests, statements of desire, inquiries* and *mentions of past experience,* actions that can be investigated across research contexts but with considerable loss of contextual nuance (from Stivers, 2002). By instead keeping an eye to moment-to-moment detail, micro-, meso- and macro-levels of analysis can be pursued in this study, linking clinician agency to social structure via the stances that they build up incrementally during interviews. I will return to the findings of these other qualitative studies during the analysis.

The analysis reveals how bodily integrity and autonomy might be compromised via pathologization at the level of social structure, but it also reveals practices of subjectivity formation and embodiment on a shorter timescale, practices also caught up in structural processes, yet giving clues to the agency of individuals. In bringing these timescales together in the analysis, Judith Butler's ethico-political construct of livability (Butler, 2004, 2015) provides a unifying framework. Livability encompasses the normative and at times violent regulation that gender can rally (i.e., its biopolitical manifestation) alongside gender as a lived and embodied experience and identity (i.e., its discursive manifestation) with the potential to rework and disrupt the normative regulation of biopolitics. In Butler's words, 'The point was precisely to relax the coercive hold of norms on gendered life – which is not the same as transcending or abolishing all norms – for the purposes of living a more liveable life' (Butler, 2015, p. 33). This point about the coercive hold of norms refers to gender's regulatory side as part of biopolitics.

I will expand on biopower in a later section, but as a temporary shorthand definition, it is a way of explaining how power works in modern nation states and refers to the subjugation and control of people, not through direct coercion of individuals, but rather by using institutions to build social practices of self-discipline into entire populations so that human biological life processes (birth, death, reproduction, illness) are managed under regimes of authority (Foucault, 1978, 2003). Biopolitics is particularly relevant for health communication, as biomedicine is a key institution in this system, and this Element explores gender's role in biopolitics in ways that illuminate the plight of intersex people while also retracing the complexity and importance of gender's roles in society.

The principal aim is to advance knowledge of how networks of structuring forces in the medical domain are in tension with the formation of subjects and bodies, shaping intersex experience and affecting access to bodily integrity and autonomy. Secondly, the analysis also uncovers broader implications for the fields of gender and language and healthcare communication. I argue that maintaining a manifold view of the processes of subject/body formation and 'biopolitics in action' is necessary as part of a re-emphasis of gender as relevant and transformative – a system of power and a lived reality. Part of this re-emphasis is a response to gender-sceptical academic arguments, but it is also a dismissal of polemical 'gender critical' (i.e., trans exclusionary) discourse, a fearmongering source of disinformation with increasingly global reach (more on this later).

In this study, I align with calls to examine my intersex project data while addressing issues of importance to intersex people themselves (Koyama and Weasel, 2002). In line with that aim and a commitment to collaborative co-mediation of knowledges and mutual benefit as ethical principles (King, 2022a, 2022b; Rowlett and King, 2023), the study will represent '[a]cademic analysis of processes by which intersex people are robbed of their bodily integrity' as called for in intersex studies (Monro et al., 2021, p. 434). For this reason, I maintain focus on socially relevant debates around patient-centred medicine in the biomedical industrial complex and the 'railroading' of parents towards biopolitical aims of eliminating 'abnormality' (as framed by socio-medical norms – Feder, 2009), with the child's individual welfare often a secondary concern or a taken-for-granted assumption.

The stigmatization of bodies with intersex variations of innate sex characteristics, and of intersex identities, by the biomedical industrial complex can lead to psychological distress and social exclusion. Efforts to support intersex individuals should focus on promoting acceptance and inclusiveness, rather than trying to 'fix' their bodies without their permission, to conform to normative gender, sexual and ableist expectations that are rooted in biopolitical forces. These forces amount to, in the words of intersex critic David Rubin, 'Western medicine's uncompromising and ultimately fatal faith in an order of things grounded in eugenic assumptions about sexual dimorphism and binary gender (2021, p. 1008)'.

I am furthermore inspired partly by the work of Orr in *Cripping Intersex* (2023) when she makes the compelling argument that one can resist pathologization and its attendant normalizing violences without reproducing ableism. Since the rise of European modernity, disability has often been understood as a biological flaw that marks certain individuals as 'abnormal' (Clare, 2017). People with disabilities have been perceived as falling short of the level of ability considered necessary to qualify as fully human. As a result, they have been cast as deviations from the norm, whose condition demands intervention by the medical-industrial system – comprising doctors, scientists, pharmaceutical experts and therapists – to correct or manage their impairments so that life becomes more bearable.

We must ask from what source the stigma emerges and how that source can be stemmed or maybe even productively diverted. Are these innate sex characteristics stigmatized via association with disability? Then again, one could argue that 'blaming' disability for the stigmatization of innate sex characteristics could represent what crip theory would call a 'stigmaphobic' stance. Alternatively, perhaps gendered/sexed ableism is doing this stigmatizing work regardless of whether innate sex characteristics are associated with, or disassociated from, disability theory. In the close analysis of clinician discourse in this study, the navigation by clinicians of ableist social norms while describing intersex variations can and will be traced.

Puar has contributed an important distinction to the critical lexicon: 'Many bodies might not be hailed as disabled but certainly are not awash in the privileges of being able-bodied either' (Puar, 2017, p. xx), a nuance she calls *debility/debilitation*, which covers unclaimed or unclaimable disabilities within the same ableist apparatus. Bodies with intersex variations are 'not hailed as disabled' but 'certainly are not awash in the privileges of being able-bodied' – they fall into neither disability nor ability and perhaps upturn the distinction, as Puar suggests. Suresh Canagarajah has also found Puar's notion of debility compelling, and he has framed it in his own crip-theory-influenced applied linguistics work to denote those who 'face limitations in lifestyle and access [to health resources] because of structural injustices' (Canagarajah, 2022, p. 28). So, although some intersex advocates have disavowed disability as too risky an association (Cornwall, 2013), intersex as a lived experience shares many characteristics with the lived experience of disability (Holmes, 2008) and so cannot easily be understood without due consideration of the ableist biopolitical apparatus. 'The fact that one is not subjected as a disabled person does not indicate that one occupies a space apart from the apparatus of disability' (Tremain, 2017, p. 23). That is, whether the label disability adheres to bodies with intersex variations and identities or not, they are also already prey to apparatuses that target 'the abnormal' for regulation.

Conforming closely to Foucault's original slant on biopolitics (Foucault, 1978, 1996, 2003), I align to the notion that sociolinguistic meaning-making is a site where biopower operates as a structural matrix, casting influence in a roundabout way via social norms, and that linguistic practices and discourses are used to regulate and control the bodies of individuals and populations, most integrally via medical power (Foucault, 1996, p. 197). This matrix is what McWhorter (2009) has described as a grid of power networks, set in motion to rid the 'human race' (read as the Nordic 'superior' standard, a subset of 'white') of all abnormality. It has been a social Darwinist project whose legacy remains formative (though often covert or latent) in the present day, fused apparatuses of gender, sex, ableism and racism (Clune-Taylor, 2020; Swarr, 2023). For this reason, to frame bodies with intersex variations in innate sex characteristics (and trans bodies although those are not the focus here) as disordered is to continue the racial arrangement of sex/gender that pathologization emerged from as part of colonialism (Meyers, 2022). Biopower also influences normalized subject formation, but it is in subjectivity processes where individual agency can have purchase. We are not, strictly speaking, dupes of biopower, and the interactional sociolinguistic discourse analysis I will conduct will permit me to zero in on the micro-level meaning-making of interview interaction to reveal the meso-level stances clinicians assemble, positioning their accounts in relation to the macro-level discourses of medical institutions and biopolitics.

The analysis in this volume demonstrates that gender, partly as an apparatus of bio/power entangled with (and inseparable from) the apparatuses of ableism (Tremain, 2017; Canagarajah, 2022) and biological sex difference (Mills, 2018), is indispensable for making sense of the bioregulation of innate sex characteristics and the consequences for bodies with intersex variations and for livability. As mentioned previously, this aim alone is of urgent importance and is the main directive of this study, yet these insights also reinforce the relevance of gender and language for everyone.

2 Intersex History and Lived Experience

Estimates vary, but a commonly cited reckoning is that one in every 2,000 babies born around the world has *visible* variations of innate sex characteristics that sit outside of biomedical and social norms, making it difficult to categorize them as male or female under social and medical belief systems (Fausto-Sterling, 2000). Where surgeons are available, most of these babies undergo surgery to make their genitalia conform to male or female social norms, in theory guiding them on a male or female life course. Nonetheless, medical ethicists have increasingly recognized that clinicians' decisions regarding sexual assignment have been based on anecdotal evidence and counterexamples (Carpenter, 2024). Indeed, analysis has shown that medical practitioners are not in consensus about the ethics of childhood 'normalizing' surgeries, which means that they do not hold the key, and medical self-reform is an unlikely pathway for resolving issues raised by intersex activists and patient advocacy organizations (Hegarty et al., 2021).

This information suggests that, for over half a century, clinicians have been making crucial choices for intersex children with little more than intuition or untrustworthy science guiding them (Kessler, 1990). This awareness has resulted in numerous alterations in healthcare legislation for intersex individuals, although these modifications are inconsistent across countries and are presently in a state of transition with little evidence of real change in healthcare (Carpenter, 2024). In response to these ethical concerns and inertia in medical practice, advocacy groups have increasingly called for permitting people with intersex variations to determine their affirmed sex during puberty or later in life. Consequently, a growing number of people are now identifying themselves as intersex, while others are self-affirming as either male or female.

In summary, there has been a biomedical quest to contain anatomical variation (Rubin, 2017), and the invisibilization of those deemed inconceivable by the sex binary via biopolitics has been a grave injustice. Before this paradoxical and disputatious situation can be fully grasped, it is important to pause and take a step back to examine the origins of these practices. It is a history of ignorance construction via what Hess (2015) calls 'undone science', or systematically produced 'non-knowledge', where research that would support the views of advocates for an abject group, or at least illuminate any claims they wish to subject to evaluation, is simply not there. In other words, this non-doing of science results in a lacuna of evidence, which is tolerated rather than prompting action, and furthermore used as a rationale for intentionally neglecting the health concerns of certain groups (Lee, 2023). In this case, the 'group' is people with intersex variations. It is also an example of a specific kind of ignorance, that which Tuana has written about in her theorizing about the production of ignorance as 'knowing that we do not know, but not caring to know' (Tuana, 2006, p. 5). But this situation has not come about accidentally, and neither is its origin a mystery lost in the mists of time. On the contrary, it is well documented to have been the contrivance of sexologists in the 1950s.

2.1 John Money and the Aftermath

In 1955, John Money, a former student of Talcott Parsons, was concerned that atypical genitals could disrupt the socialization process of intersex children and their learning of gender roles (Karkazis, 2008; Reis, 2009). He theorized that gender was a psychosocial state representing one's masculine or feminine identity, which formed a permanently 'closed system' during a critical period in the first eighteen months of life (Morland, 2015). Money believed surgery could help establish a binary gender role (e.g., boy or girl) based on genital appearance (Morland, 2015). He thought children were highly adaptable during this critical period, but having genitals that did not match their gender of rearing could lead to social and psychological difficulties. Despite knowing full well that most intersex adults without surgery were content with their bodies (Repo, 2016), Money's concern was rooted in what he perceived to be potential disruption to the nuclear family, allegedly to be caused by non-conformity of bodies with intersex variations (Repo, 2016; Malatino, 2019). His research destabilized the idea of sex as unitary but used gender to reinforce binary sex in medicine (Rubin, 2017). This effort made bodies with intersex variations more governable, leading to anatomical regulation through genital surgery. Money's ideas, which remain entrenched in global biomedicine, regulate bodies with intersex variations at an individual level to maintain population-level control. Although his core premise that infant genital surgery is necessary to keep gender identity stable lacked strong scientific support, his recommended procedures continue to be widely used as outlined in the previous section, resulting in consequences, often grave, for intersex people's lives. Along the way, there have also been disputes around terminology, a topic that merits review because the various terms will arise in the data, and it is important to understand each term's sociopolitical loading.

2.2 Terminology and Bodies with Intersex Variations

Historically, the term intersex was employed in biomedicine (from 1917 to 2006) as a diagnostic classification, ostensibly gradually replacing the term 'hermaphrodite', a term that was becoming controversial in medicine (Holmes, 2009). In the early 1990s, the terms and concepts of intersex were first appropriated by activists in the US and Australia (Carpenter, 2016), strategically removing their medical connotations (Jenkins and Short, 2017) and embracing intersex as a positive divergence from societal expectations (Holmes, 2011). Many people with intersex variations use the term intersex, while others do not, with some using it to describe their identity, body traits, or presumably both (Davis, 2015; Lundberg, Hegarty, and Roen, 2018). Numerous surveys across Europe, Australia and the US have indicated that they found scarcely any people with intersex variations or their family members who were willing to use the disorders of sex development (DSD) language (Hegarty and Lundberg, 2020). In an Australian study of individuals with minoritized sex traits, 60 per cent identified as intersex, but only 20 per cent as gender non-binary (Carpenter, 2018). The survey did not clarify whether they referred to their body or identity as intersex, or both, leaving unanswered questions. However, all this information confirms that there is no straightforward link between non-binary gender identity and bodies with intersex variations.

In response to the demedicalization of 'intersex', Western medicine largely discarded the term, adopting DSD as a new diagnostic category in 2006 as part of the Chicago 'consensus' statement (Carpenter, 2016; King, Dayrell, and Zorzi, 2026). Since its introduction, qualitative research from the US context indicates that the DSD label has received mixed reactions among individuals with intersex variations, considered helpful for medical discussions but problematic in its implication of abnormality (Davis, 2015). In contrast, the medical discourse community, especially in the Global North and extending beyond the US to the UK and Europe (Pasterski, Prentice and Hughes, 2010), has embraced the term without hesitation, reestablishing bioregulatory control over bodies and reaffirming their authority to manage, 'correct' and 'align' these bodies with societal expectations rather than embracing their uniqueness (Holmes, 2009). This has led to the renewed silencing of those affected by the diagnosis (Holmes, 2011).

2.3 Hegemonies of Science and Zombie Facts

It has now long been argued that the biopolitics around intersex variations are deeply entwined with social norms and social practices surrounding gender and sexuality. Commentators have convincingly demonstrated that medical interventions to 'normalize' bodies through surgeries and hormone treatments are often driven by a desire to conform to binary *gender* categories and enforce heteronormative norms (Karkazis, 2008; Feder, 2014). What is also clear is that ableism and racism are also bound up with gender and sex in the construction of these bodies as abnormality. However, when justifying medical interventions, various scientific discourses have been drawn upon, but they are grounded in neither evidence-based medicine nor up-to-date biological science.

The idea of 'hormonal sex' (i.e., that testosterone makes boys, and oestrogen makes girls), although familiar to many and still bandied about, was long ago debunked (Oudshoorn, 1990; Jordan-Young and Karkazis, 2019). It was then replaced as a binary benchmark by neurocognitive 'brain sex' whereby women and men were framed as having substantially different brain structures due to hormonal exposures in utero (also now firmly debunked – Jordan-Young, 2010). Subsequently, hopes for the binary were 'piously' salvaged by turning to the idea of chromosomal sex (i.e., the Y chromosome makes boys). But, as the science historian Rosario has put it, 'advances in the genetics of sex determination have completely trashed the 1950s notion that the human Y chromosome alone determines sex' (Rosario, 2009, p. 274). This has not stopped the biomedical establishment from clinging in their discourse to what Griffiths (2018) has called promissory genetics, which rests on *futurism*, in this case the belief that future developments in genetic science will resolve the uncertainty of bodily variation. Rosario himself placed hope (for a future turn *away* from such unreflective lookstep binary thinking) in clear evidence that sex emerges out of 'a quantum cloud of biological and environmental effects' (Rosario, 2009, p. 279) and is far from simply binary. There is constant feedback between the body and social experiences, a dynamic interplay of the social and the biological over time in a composite of nature and nurture, not a binary contest (Fausto-Sterling, 2005, 2008). However, it has since emerged that, undeterred by molecular genetic evidence that there is no simple binary, biologists have turned their attention to 'genomic sex' in their quest for a binary explanation in a different dichotomy; that is, every cell in a male body is different from every cell in a female body at the genomic level (Richardson, 2013; Sanz, 2017). The findings of this latest effort have provided little comfort to those hoping for clear definitions of binary sex (Fausto-Sterling, 2012; Karkazis, 2019). Dimorphism self-perpetuates in a hegemonic game of shifting goal posts.

So, biological sex dimorphism is an unproven biological assumption that suggests a clear division between male and female mammals, with any other forms considered abnormalities (Rosario, 2009; Rubin, 2016; Hutton, 2019). In truth, mammalian bodies exhibit a range of sexual traits (Hutton, 2019), and humans are no different, with some intersex variations perhaps more *salient*, leading to their classification as pathological. There is no biological basis for categorizing intersex characteristics as abnormal (Hutton, 2019). Nonetheless, the notion of human exceptionalism seems to persist in the field of human biology (King, 2022a). Orr refers to the 'institutionalization of the epistemological fiction of sex dimorphism' as 'compulsory dyadism' (2023, p. 20) and points out that ableism drives this instance of human exceptionalism. Eckert (2017), on the other hand, aligns with Butler (1993), arguing that this hegemony of dimorphism is driven by the fact that sex is always already gender, suggesting that as long as we keep trying to work with the gender/sex split, dimorphism will enter via the backdoor despite our best intentions.

'Science' is often evoked as a 'commonsense' justification for treating the two-sex model as the truth and all else as theory or sophistry, thus erroneously (and naively) *inverting* the truth, which is that science has in fact *ruled out* simplistic notions of human sex, leaving these notions in the dustbin of history as incontrovertibly obsolete constructs (Richardson, 2013; Hutton, 2019). Delimata (2019) has written a book-length exposé of the entrenched assumptions that have made non-dimorphic sex variance seem unnatural. She cites Jablonka and Lamb (2005), pointing out that the view of the gene as a simple, causal agent, as often forwarded by non-geneticist scientists and journalists (and increasingly politicians), is fundamentally outdated and invalid. Genes do not constitute the essence of an organism despite popular belief, since that organism is the product of a complex system of genes, cells and environment. Genotypes do not necessarily lead to particular phenotypes (Delimata, 2019).

Moreover, even the update to the 2006 'Chicago consensus' statement, an update written by an international and multidisciplinary 'consortium' of clinicians, puts it quite plainly that genetics alone remains unable to explain the biology of 'DSDs' [i.e., intersex variations] (Lee et al., 2016). However, former 'facts' about genes (i.e., zombie facts) have been slow to filter out of medical discourse, and those committed to dimorphism tend to animate outdated stancetaking about sex and biology:

> Those questioning simplistic understandings of sex – scientists among them – are hardly unscientific, but rather keen observers of the science of sex biology and the peculiar categorical gate-keeping of, say, soldiers and elite women athletes. This is not a case of science versus social constructionism as some argue; it's about the calculated use of "biological sex" to buttress obsolete thinking about sex (Karkazis, 2019, p. 1899).

The obsolete aspects include any notion that sex is simply and straightforwardly molecular in origin and binary, with biological science providing no easy-to-administer definitions (at the time of writing) of either sex or gender, whether one is discussing humans or the broader membership of class *Mammalia* (Fausto-Sterling, 2012; Swarr, 2023). These are what Jordan-Young and Karkazis (2019, p. 77) have called 'zombie facts', referring to now overruled (i.e., dead) facts that continue to live on no matter how many times they are disproved (often disproved even by the very researchers whose work lent them the status of fact in the first place). A number of zombie facts raise their ragged heads and stagger into the middle of stancetaking processes during the coming analysis. There are also inconclusive notions circulating in discourse (basically hypotheses) about genomic sex rescuing the binary (Sanz, 2017), but all are based on an assumption that is never questioned – that sex is binary – and so it goes round and round, as a circle has no beginning.

3 Biopolitics and Gender in Sociolinguistics

During interactional sociolinguistic discourse analysis, gender, a multidimensional system of power, cannot be separated from contemporary technologies of the body and bioregulation, which sit at the centre of biopolitics. For Foucault, practices in daily life are central to relations of power, and Gumperz gave us empirical tools and procedures in interactional sociolinguistics for understanding these practices at the site of their performance, showing commensurability between a Foucauldian biopolitical critical orientation and discourse analysis inspired by interactional sociolinguistics (Rampton, 2016; Borba, 2019). It is in biopolitics, wherein some bodies are disciplined to fit racial capitalism (McWhorter, 2009), or 'subject to capture by biomedical gender regulation' (Wolff, Rubin and Swarr, 2022, p. 145), while others are 'killable or cageable' (Ellison et al., 2017, p. 164) because they are 'surplus' to it. In other words, certain 'abnormal' bodies face direct biomedical intervention to make them more useful, while others are written off as neglectable or disposable because they are beyond 'repair'.

Ruminating on transgender experience, substantively different from intersex experience yet still instructive, Susan Stryker has said:

> Transgender phenomena – anything that calls our attention to the contingency and unnaturalness of gender normativity – appear at the margins of the biopolitically operated-upon body, at those fleeting and variable points at which particular bodies exceed or elude capture within the gender apparatus when they defy the logic of the biopolitical calculus or present a case that confounds an administrative rule or bureaucratic practice (Stryker, 2014, p. 40).

In other words, by merely existing, certain bodies expose the distortions upon which dominant (i.e., binary) beliefs about gender rest, and so in turn upset policies undergirded by those beliefs. By paying attention to gender as an apparatus, to how subjects are captured by it or exceed or elude it, as Stryker says in the quotation, we can explore biopolitical practices while still using gender as an analytical tool for critique. What can gender-informed biopolitical analysis tell us about viability and livability?

3.1 Gender

One of my aims in this Element, which sits alongside the foremost aim of querying biomedical discourse about bodies with intersex variations, is to begin exploring the relationship between gender and biopolitics while also examining the claims of Foucauldian gender sceptics. I refer to claims about the limitations of gender's emancipatory potential (e.g., Repo, 2016; Eckert, 2017) and what these claims might mean for language and gender. These sceptical claims stem from anxieties that by thinking with gender we might unwittingly be reproducing its biopolitical and normalizing functions during analysis of phenomena such as clinician accounts of their talk around intersex variations.

These ostensible limitations of gender for feminism have long been discussed (Scott, 1996; Lorber, 2021), and the associated debate between feminists of various sub-movements over whether gender as a concept continues to be useful is not a new debate. As Karhu aptly put it recently, 'criticisms of gender as a liberating concept or identity (e.g., queer criticisms of identity politics) are a standard point of departure in Foucauldian influenced queer and trans theorizations' (Karhu, 2022, p. 303, n11). So, logic suggests that if we 'keep our wits about us', it becomes possible to avoid 'unwittingly' reproducing the conservative, regulatory version of gender (i.e., the biopolitical apparatus) set in motion by John Money and colleagues in the 1950s. We can take advantage of feminist and queer scholarship that shows the criss-crossing qualities of gender as concurrently normalizing and resistive, bound up in the gender order as a system of power. We can also inspect how the pernicious effects of gender as a biopolitical apparatus are shaped partly by societal institutions such as biomedicine as much as discourse. Interactional sociolinguistic discourse analysis of language and stancetaking in the interview accounts will permit me to track the crossing points between these processes.

Indeed, queer linguistics, in its relatively recent explorations of discursive practices around certainty and uncertainty in gender normativity, '... confirms the limits of gender as an explanatory category' when it is assumed to be a static binary (Leap, 2012, p. 558). In other words, we have learned that it is normative assumptions about binarity itself that limit gender's ability to enlighten us (Davis, Zimman, and Raclaw, 2014). Yet this obstacle need not lead to scepticism about the usefulness of gender as a concept. Its relevance does not rest on being theorized as some kind of 'model' that explains the social world. Gender is instead a raft of *processes* that *defy* being wedged into such a set of static categories via abstract, decontextualised description (Leap, 2023). For these reasons, queer linguistics takes acute interest in interrogating structures of normative authority and regulatory power (Leap, 2015). That is, queer linguistics treats gender as a system of normativity and regulation, but also a *lived reality* that can contest and destabilize the 'truth' of any sense of normality that has accrued around binary gender (and sexuality) and notions of how to talk about it (Milani, 2014, 2018). As such it is a more accurately Butlerian sense of gender (Karhu, 2022) that structures and resists, requiring from interactional sociolinguistic analysis what Tommaso Milani has referred to as 'a fine-grained mapping of the complex interplay of norms, and forms of resistance to them, in specific domains of practice' (2018, p. 18), and so it is a stance highly compatible with the concept of biopolitics and the micro-analytical approach I have outlined.

3.1.1 Why Double Down on Gender?

We can create a more sophisticated notion of gender as emancipatory *and* regulatory *and* lived reality. As Bonnie McElhinney put it twenty years ago, '"Gender" retains significance for people living their lives, not just people analysing how people live their lives' (McElhinney, 2003, p. 30). Gender normativities bind people to the objectives of biomedical reasoning and biopolitical responsibility in both enabling and constraining ways (Mohr, 2019). If we are to agree that gender is a variable in the management of populations, both in its sexological and feminist deployments (Repo, 2016), and no longer (if ever) just a device that helps with the analysis and critique of society but also a device through which the governance of individuals ensues, then it is gender as a system of power that must be included in our focus – a historicized version of gender better equipped to deal with its violent normalizing origins while still being liberatory in the present as a critical tool and a lived reality through which to exercise self-determination (Karhu, 2022). It is a 'gender' that cannot be separated from biopolitics. As Karhu (2022, p. 314) has said concerning trans-affirmative feminism, it must be a feminism 'that takes seriously the normalizing discourses of gender but recognizes and affirms the disobedient ways gender is currently being lived – and contested'. It is this dichotomy that points to liveable lives for people with intersex variations, as gender plays both roles in the discourses of healthcare communication.

In resisting the idea that anatomy is destiny, most feminist sub-movements have rejected biological determinism (Birke, 1999), and this rejection has been an epistemological cornerstone of the gender and language field (Mills and Mullany, 2011). However, in this Element I will assert that bringing biopolitics and gender together, as commensurable notions, does not entail returning to biologism. Incorporating analysis of biopolitics in action using interactional sociolinguistics is a compatible way to examine the meeting place between macro (structure) and micro (agency).

3.1.2 Gender Scepticism

Gender as a system of power is still relevant in biopolitics, or, as Repo (2016) argues, it is a biopolitical apparatus itself. Furthermore, Repo (2016, p. 147) has argued that gender emerged as a key concept 'around which the psychiatric, economic, and demographic discourses regulating sexual difference converged over the past decades, resulting in the deployment of gender in disciplinary, biopolitical and neoliberal discourses, practices and contexts' (Repo, 2016, p. 147). Repo thus retraces gender as a historically specific apparatus of biopower and calls into question the emancipatory potential of the category in feminist theory and politics. It behoves language and gender scholarship to begin engaging with this debate. However, it is important to remember that gender does not need to be kept separate from other social forces. As Rubin puts it, '[W]hatever story we tell about gender, that story is never gender's alone. It is always also a story about science and technology, the centrality of race to modern sexual classificatory schema, the making of the normal and the natural, and the failures and violences of liberal humanism' (Rubin, 2022, pp. 182–183). Indeed, the intertwined *stories* of gender, biological science, biomedical technologies, and social norms of class, dis/ability, as well as institutional norms and biopolitical apparatuses, will all be seen to play a role in the interview accounts of clinicians in Hong Kong. It is in the incremental stance development, constructed of their discursive moves, that I aim to trace how it all coexists and inflects, affecting the lived experiences of people with intersex variations and their families.

Repo, evoking Audre Lorde, has positioned gender as the 'master's tool' that has met its limits and lost its critical edge due to changing circumstances whereby neoliberal governmentality's 'unrelenting appropriative powers' (Repo, 2016, p. 178) have sapped it of its potency, and new tools are required. My aim here is not to deny that gender (as a concept, process and lived reality) has been generated (and lived) in a chequered history within (neo)liberalism; I hope it is obvious that I see this problematic history as crucial to my own understanding of gender. Rather, my intention is to assert that acknowledging this shortcoming need not entail throwing our hands up in horror and retreating from gender. It requires a critical re-articulation of gender, a possibility that gets disregarded in the gender-sceptical haste to discard it (Karhu, 2022). Although Money narrowly preceded feminist writers by being the first to appropriate the term gender from linguistics, more liberatory ideas about gender and discourse from some influential feminist quarters developed on separate trajectories, unfettered by Money's sexological conservatism. These histories do not cancel one another out, nor does gender in its biopolitical apparatus form (i.e., as a structural system of power) erase the fact that the biopower of gender creates hope in 'the complex interplay of norms, and forms of resistance to them, in specific domains of practice' (Milani, 2018, p. 18). It is a muscular hope, or what Silva and Borba (2024) have recently labelled as *esperançar*, a Brazilian Portuguese neologism of 'to hope' linked in lore to the wordplay of Paulo Freire, which is framed by the authors not as passive waiting, escapism or pious futurism, but as a 'muscle' for pragmatic and reflexive action.

So, how emancipatory is gender? Intersex critic David Rubin captures its multidimensional qualities in the following words: 'Recalling with Foucault that there is no outside to power relations, and recognizing that gender is not merely a repressive technology but also a productive one, the challenge is to imagine strategies for expressing human potential in ways that can *embrace uncertainty and enhance practices of freedom* without consolidating the psychosomatic harms of gender regulation' (Rubin, 2017, p. 44, *my emphasis*). I take this to mean that gender can play a role in liberating people (such as people with intersex variations) even while we acknowledge its problematic regulatory side. As a result, I take Foucauldian gender sceptics seriously, though our positions differ. A more sophisticated concept of gender can emerge through incorporating biopower and biopolitics and from a considered response to Foucauldian feminist critiques, a reasoned response that changes course from pessimism towards *esperançar* – hope as pragmatic and reflexive action.

3.1.3 Gender-Critical Feminism and the Far Right

It is also very important in this Element for me to be unequivocal that, in taking gender-sceptical Foucauldian scholars seriously, I at the same time have no truck with the far-right anti-gender movement and its anti-gender discourse, originating with the Vatican and circulating the globe, vilifying gender as apocalyptic (Case, 2019) via bamboozlement and misrepresentation (Borba, Hall and Hiramoto, 2020; Gal, 2021; Borba, 2022; Zottola and Borba, 2022). I align with the idea that right-wing anti-gender discourse is akin to a pathogen infecting the world and requires a linguistic 'public health' response (Russell, 2023).

Neither do I engage with 'gender-critical feminism', which is essentially the latest iteration of a resurgent trans antagonism (Malatino, 2021), or another way to put it is ' . . . old transphobia dressed up in new terminology' (Zimman, 2021, p. 427). Furthermore, gender-critical feminists and the far right find themselves echoing one another in many cases, not because they share a common ideal of womanhood, for they do not, but primarily because both ideologies prop up a white supremacist worldview (Barrett and Hall, 2023). As I have argued elsewhere, the parallel historical development of racism on the one hand and the pathologization of bodies with intersex variations on the other hand (along with trans bodies, though a separate issue), 'cannot be separated, each one propping up the other' (King, 2023a). Rosa and Flores have endorsed my stance on biopower, agreeing that biopolitical analysis can shed light on the 'joint production and governance of phenomena such as race, language, gender, sexuality, labour, and ability as modes of population management that reflect the mutually constitutive nature of capitalism and colonialism' (Rosa and Flores, 2023, p. 484). They suggest that this is an important insight that can 'help move beyond liberal humanist orientations to identities as discrete demographic categories that are individually embodied and practiced' (Rosa and Flores, 2023, p. 484). In this way, we are better prepared to notice the evidence of joint productions and forms of governance, what I frame as 'biopolitics in action', in all levels of our data.

3.2 Biopower and Biopolitics

Foucault's concept of biopolitics examines how power operates to foster, sustain and expand life, making living itself the central concern of governance.

He frames biopolitics as integral to the formation of subjectivities, with race, sex/gender and disability functioning as key axes through which life is regulated and experienced (Mills, 2018). For Foucault, biopolitics is not only about control or repression; it is also inherently productive, creating possibilities for life and shaping the very meaning of living. This shifts biopower beyond the older sovereign right to decide who lives or dies, toward a focus on power's capacity to produce life in diverse forms (Giroux, 2008).

Although Foucault recognises a division within biopower between those who must live and those who must die, he resists the more pessimistic emphasis on death and abandonment found in later theorists such as Agamben and Mbembe. His model preserves a tension between productive and repressive forces, leaving room for resistance and hope, and recognising the influence of non-state actors on biopolitical processes (McWhorter, 1999). This openness makes his framework valuable for critically analysing healthcare communication, where discourse not only reflects established norms but also contains potential for transformation. Such an outlook supports a sociolinguistics of *esperançar* – understood here as hope cultivated actively, as a capacity for action (see Section 3.1.2).

Building on Foucault, Giorgio Agamben develops a more legalistic, state-focused approach, concentrating on sovereign authority over life and death. His notion of the 'state of exception' describes situations in which sovereign power suspends normal legal protections, reducing certain people to 'bare life', or life exposed to death and abandonment (Agamben, 1995, 2005). Critics argue that this perspective, with its emphasis on repression and dystopian overtones, offers limited insight in contexts where resistance, agency and diffuse power relations are apparent (Lemke, 2005).

Achille Mbembe extends the discussion by introducing necropolitics, which centres on the role of death and racialised violence in governing populations (Mbembe, 2019). His analysis highlights the ways biopolitical systems enforce hierarchies that determine who suffers and dies, placing colonial and postcolonial histories at the forefront. Like Agamben, Mbembe's reading prioritises themes of abandonment and fatality over productive or resistant capacities.

Roberto Esposito advances the field further through the opposition between community and immunity. He argues that biopolitical regimes establish immunitary mechanisms, or protective systems that safeguard some groups by exposing or excluding others. In his view, the politics of care and protection cannot be separated from the politics of exclusion and violence, especially in healthcare and policy arenas (Esposito, 2008). This framework offers a bridge between Foucault's emphasis on the generative aspects of life and Agamben's focus on sovereign power and mortality, illustrating how inclusion and exclusion jointly define lived experience.

Overall, while Agamben and Mbembe deepen biopolitical theory by stressing its sovereign and necropolitical dimensions, and Esposito articulates the interplay between care and exclusion, Foucault's original formulation remains the most practically effective for analysing healthcare communication. By balancing power's productive and repressive elements and acknowledging the roles of non-state actors and resistance, his approach enables a critical and hopeful engagement with the normative and transformative potentials within biopolitical systems.

3.2.1 Fused Biopolitical Apparatuses

Returning to Repo's critique of gender in biopolitics, as Mills (2018, p. 172) points out, 'Repo takes it as given that sexual difference is something to be regulated, rather than a regulatory device in itself', and this assumption evades the possibility that biological sex difference is itself a biopolitical apparatus, and one in urgent need of critical analysis (see also Karhu, 2022). Foucault saw biological sex as the most speculative element in the deployment of sexuality in biopower, not the material anchor-point of sexuality (Mills, 2018, p. 170). Mills asks, is sexual difference the most 'ideal' (i.e., speculative) element of the deployment of gender? If so, then sexual difference is itself a biopolitical apparatus, a notion supported by the analysis of Meyers (2022), who convincingly traces the racialized history of the disorder framework to demonstrate that race and sex/gender are entangled in that apparatus. 'Biological sex' was, from its foundational moments, racialized into differing categories with Black people perceived as the least sexually dimorphic and white people the most sexually dimorphic (Markowitz, 2001), which fed into the whiteness of infant surgical sex assignment (Meyers, 2022).

Mills (2018) counters Repo's contention that gender has regulated sexual difference by arguing that sexual difference did not need gender to be binary – rather, Darwinian notions of sex complementarity, epistemologically baked into biology and so into biopower, had already achieved it. That is, Darwin's discussion of dyadic sexual difference being integral to species survival was merely one take on sexual difference, but in human biology as an emerging field of knowledge/power it became reified as a manifestation of nature, becoming central to the normalization of sexed bodies despite the obvious variety that lay between the bifurcated categories (i.e., bodies with intersex variations) (Grosz, 2004). Although Mills does not generate a complete genealogy of sexual difference, she argues convincingly that this entrenchment of binary sexual difference in biology points to sexual difference itself as another regulatory apparatus in biopolitics, not simply being regulated by gender as part of biopower, as suggested by Repo. The two are co-constitutive biopolitical apparatuses along with race and ableism (Mills, 2018).

Then again, there are more components to Repo's genealogy of gender. She writes about the rise of the gender concept post-world wars, and the renewed problematizations of reproductive life: 'Culture, society, and personality, encapsulated in the idea of gender, ascended to a more important status than sex, now understood as the merely biological side of reproduction which gender worked to realize' (2016, p. 132). Gender 'endowed' sex with competence via a thinking subject that could be socialized into sexual behaviour patterns as part of neoliberal governmentality in biopolitics. In this way she justifies the notion that gender has regulated biological sex and sexual difference, weaving gender into Foucault's positioning of sexuality as the 'hinge' of biopolitics. These arguments are quite convincing as far as they go, showing that gender is bound up in biopolitics. Yet part of this socialization emergence for Repo was the spreading of the bioregulatory aspect of Money's intersex treatment regime into feminism via appropriation of his gender concept. He created the notion of gender role as one's fixed, separate, postnatally developed psychosocial personality, a formulation which Repo, rightly, is very hard on key feminist thinkers for being insufficiently critical about as they deployed the idea of gender to liberate women while leaving intersex and trans subjects abject. Repo points out that the appropriating feminist writers either did so through silence about that pathologization (e.g., Kate Millet) or through endorsing it (e.g., Germaine Greer). Repo leans heavily on this murky and arguably dishonourable history in her questioning of gender's usefulness to feminism. What gets missed in her exposé is the fact that Money's stance was interactionist, neither purely biologically deterministic nor purely socially constructionist (Oakley, 1972; Sullivan, 2015). This means that he still saw biological sex as playing a key role and not completely in the thrall of gender.

Not a surgeon himself, Money drew on his understanding of 'humanist' psychology of the period (e.g., Adler, Maliniak, Parsons) to rationalize surgery as a means to facilitate lived experiences, instigated through genital appearance, that would precipitate a binary gender role as either man or woman (Morland, 2015). In other words, he theorized that an intersex baby can be raised as a girl but if not living subjectively in a female body she might not feel like a girl, undoing her (socially engineered) gendering. Gender and biological sex (the latter at least in terms of phenotype, or the complex outward expression of genetics) are clearly interacting in his theory despite the power that he and his colleagues indisputably instilled in gender as a psychosocial trait. This point is important for the current study because in the analysis of the clinicians' accounts, we will see that biological sex regulates gender as much as is the reverse. This finding has led me to align with Mills to argue that sexual difference is as much a biopolitical apparatus as gender is, and they are mutually reinforcing, or as McWhorter put it in her genealogy of race and sexuality in 'Anglo-America', they are 'historically codependent and mutually determinative' (McWhorter, 2009, p. 14). Their mutually determinative nature will be seen in my analysis, brought into view by the subtleties and nuances of stancetaking analysis.

3.3 Bringing Gender and Biopolitics Together

In bringing the gender and biopolitics together theoretically, it must be asked what does each offer? And what does the synthesis of the two achieve that is relevant to the questions at hand concerning intersex variations? I align to Stryker's stance (2014) that 'gender' has already proved to be in accord with Foucault's theorizing of biopolitics, and we can productively build on that synergy in studies of language, gender and power, opening up new vistas for research. Gender in biopolitics does not pertain primarily to questions of representation; rather, such processes are secondary yet very important (McWhorter, 1999; Stryker, 2014). It is instead ' ... an apparatus within which all bodies are taken up, which creates material effects through bureaucratic tracking that begins with birth, ends with death' (Stryker, 2014, p. 39). Gender is thus an integral part of the mechanism through which power moulds a given population via a set of administrative structures and practices.

It is as Pennycook has been reminding linguists, while drawing on the work of Luke (2013) and Latour (2004); discursive analysis of representation and material analysis of the state and political economy are complimentary and intertwined, neither one cancelling out the other *and both causative of the other* (Pennycook, 2022). This point is fundamental to my analysis because, through the accounts of these Hong Kong clinicians, evidence of ideologies emerges from their discursive representations of innate sex characteristics and parent subjectivities. It would be naïve to suggest that these ideologies are only influencing their *discourse*. Rather, the ideologies identified are bound to be influencing their other practices, and the practices of parents, who are influenced directly by clinicians in the action chains of patient-centred medicine when reworked for paediatric contexts.

4 Research Context, Design and Method

4.1 Hong Kong

4.1.1 Geopolitics and Colonialism

Hong Kong, a region that has long defied simple categorization as either a centre or periphery (So and Kwok, 1995), spent approximately 150 years as a British crown colony and dependent territory before becoming a 'special administrative region' of China in 1997 under the 'one country, two systems' policy. This arrangement granted Hong Kong a degree of autonomy, which has recently been curtailed (Lo, 2021). These curtailments have not had any relevant impact on medical practices in relation to this study. However, the colonial history of the territory does have relevance, for the history of *western medicine* in Hong Kong predictably has a colonial legacy.

4.1.2 Medicine in Hong Kong

The first seventy-odd years of colonial rule were a period in which both the British and the Chinese in Hong Kong had predominantly looked at each other's medical knowledge and practices with mutual disrespect bordering on horror (Chan-Yeung, 2018). However, views slowly evolved, and starting in 1910, a rapid shift occurred with the founding of the University of Hong Kong and its faculty of medicine. Even though cultural prejudices were still present, a mixture of altruism and opportunistic self-interest brought Hong Kong to where it is now, a century later, as a place known for state-of-the-art Western medicine alongside traditional Chinese medicine, which also enjoys acknowledgement (Chan-Yeung, 2018). So, although, as stated previously, Hong Kong is problematic to categorize as centre or periphery in global geopolitics, biomedically it is tightly in step with the centre. This insight also applies to innate sex characteristics and pathologization. The Hong Kong medical system has also remained largely in step with the move to patient-centred care, following the UK in a shift of the balance of power to greater involvement of patients in healthcare decision-making (Lau, 2002).

4.1.3 Patient-Centred Medicine

Patient-centred medicine is an approach to healthcare that prioritizes the individual needs, values and preferences of the patient, integrating them into clinical decision-making and treatment planning (Edgman-Levitan and Schoenbaum, 2021). Unlike traditional models that focus primarily on disease and biomedical outcomes, patient-centred medicine emphasizes holistic care, active listening, shared decision-making and respect for patient autonomy. This approach exists because research has shown that engaging patients in their care improves satisfaction, adherence to treatment and overall health outcomes (Rathert, Wyrwich, and Boren, 2013). It is a model that has become hegemonic and taken for granted, originally developed to position patients as more autonomous but evolving (problematically) to position them as resources or even treatment-team members (Siouta and Olsson, 2020). Finally, there are clinician-acknowledged paradoxes in conducting 'patient' centred care when a guardian is the surrogate decision maker. Paediatric patients very often cannot participate in their own medical decisions, so surrogates (parents) make decisions for them, guided by the 'best interest standard'. Parents' preferences must be elicited but then *evaluated* for whether they truly serve the child's best interests. This can undermine building authentic consensus because it recentres clinician authority, differing sharply from adult patient-centred encounters (Opel, 2017). These nuances will become relevant during the analysis of clinician accounts in this study.

4.1.4 English and Cantonese

While Cantonese is undeniably the dominant language for most people in most domains, English (and increasingly Standard Mandarin, or Putonghua) also plays a role, with English holding significant symbolic and practical value as an official language (Yeung and Gray, 2023). This multilingual setting, characterized by differences in the usage of Cantonese and English, results in a plurilingual interaction where Cantonese is the primary language, but English words are often incorporated through context-specific instances of 'transference' or as borrowed terms that have been somewhat integrated into Cantonese (Li, 2017). Transferring English words can occur due to temporary memory lapses, perceived or actual gaps in Cantonese vocabulary, or when a known Cantonese equivalent is considered 'semantically incongruent and therefore unusable from the speaker's or writer's perspective' (Li, 2017, p. 29). For example, English's prevalence in education has led to the frequent incorporation of English academic or technical terms (Li, 2017), which can be observed in the data presented. It is well documented that relegating a local language (like Cantonese) into a state of erasure in the education system can lead to linguistic inequalities (Bonnin, 2013; Phyak and Sah, 2024). This language economy in Hong Kong, with English in a key economic role and a marker of education level and social class, is a manifestation of linguistic governmentality. That is, linguistic conduct is not forced but guided as part of controlling the population through governance of themselves (Yeung and Gray, 2023). As the analysis will reveal, recruiting parents and patients to be biopolitical managers of intersex variations, and moulding them as parent subjects, is intricately tied to this language economy of Cantonese and English, and so biopower and language are connected.

4.2 Recruitment of Interviewees

The data for this study has been selected from transcriptions of research interviews[2] with medical practitioners in Hong Kong who work closely with

---

[2] Thank you to Leung Hin Ming (Matthew) for transcribing and translating and Putsalun Chhim for interviewing, transcribing and translating.

children and adults with intersex variations and their families. The clinicians interviewed were recruited through a key participant identified by my contacts in the Faculty of Medicine at the University of Hong Kong as a leader among clinicians in the territory who engage as part of their duties with relevant patients and their families. Via this doctor's network, word was spread that I was conducting this study on the language used to discuss innate sex characteristics with parents and patients. I was contacted by twelve clinicians (a mix of physicians and surgeons) whose specializations included endocrinology, urology and gynaecology. My research assistant and I interviewed them after they signed consent forms.

4.3 Research Design and Method

4.3.1 Data Collection – Interviews

We conducted the interviews in late 2021, partly in English and partly in Cantonese, with the Cantonese portions translated into English prior to the analysis presented here. For reasons of ethical research practice, I have changed all names of the clinicians, as interviewees, to pseudonyms, and I have avoided mention of their medical specialization and even their gender unless either was made relevant by the interviewee in the recorded interview and bore relevance in answering the research questions. Because there are very few medical professionals doing this work in Hong Kong, I decided that this extra level of identity protection was ethically necessary.

The interviews were semi-structured and focused on the topic of talk about bodies with intersex variations. However, it became evident early in the research project that the clinicians' shared definition of 'intersex' was at odds with broader definitions used by the international intersex activist community. This means they have joined with their medical peers internationally in strategically compartmentalizing intersex variations into a very narrow band of embodiments, enabling them to suggest that they do not treat intersex per se via surgeries; rather, they only treat very specific 'disorders' (Davis and Preves, 2020). This narrowing amounts to a disingenuous evasion because, in short, the prevalence of infant genital surgeries on children worldwide, including in Hong Kong, remains largely unchanged (Carpenter, 2016). This discursive and classificatory strategy of avoidance will be noticeable during this study's analysis. Still, it seemed unwise to achieve the inclusiveness I desired by sparring with them over categories, for such a conversation was unlikely to be fruitful. To side-step this disputatious minefield and get at the desired topic, it turned out the best strategy was to avoid disputed terms, opting for a descriptive approach. Questions required the interviewees to reflect on how they would refer to and describe a person's innate sex characteristics that were deemed 'medical' in nature. In other words, the person had become a 'patient' because of their innate sex characteristics. This way of stating who fits in the category also avoids incendiary terms like 'pathologized', at least during interviews.

4.3.2 Data Analysis – An Interactional Sociolinguistic Approach

As mentioned in earlier sections, the approach I deploy is discourse analysis grounded in interactional sociolinguistics, focusing on language use during interviews. I treat the interviews as social interactions, an approach that does not treat participants' words as simply communicating individual experience plainly and transparently; rather, transparent or not, their words amount to discourse, accomplishing social actions and negotiating stances and identities. This type of analysis keeps two levels of speech in view, that of the habitually performed form and substance of their speech as they give accounts (neither apprehended nor intended consciously), but also at the highly salient meta level of communication. It is sometimes characterized as 'talk about talk'.

Interactional sociolinguistic discourse analysis, as I deploy it in this study, enables me to undertake my stated aim of paying attention to gender as an apparatus, to how subjects are captured by it or exceed or elude it, and to how we can explore biopolitical practices while still using gender as an analytical tool for critique. Furthermore, it enables analysis that reveals insights about the viability and livability of lives for people with intersex variations and their family members, addressing reasons for sober reflection and *esperançar* (hope as a muscle for action). It does so by permitting a microanalysis of meaning-making practices, bridging spoken accounts, stance taking, social norms, and institutional norms to uncover a complex web of evaluation, affiliation, detachment and resistance in the biomedical domain. Stances affect relationships between people and relations to the 'objects' and content being constructed in talk. Therefore, close analysis of the clinicians' stancetaking processes gives us access to moments in which biopolitics is instantiated and gender plays certain roles in animation of the stances circulating in society, the authoring of personal stances, and the communication of degrees of investment in a stance. What, then, do I mean by stancetaking?

Stance and Stancetaking

Taking stances is every speaker's main interest in an interaction and is of central importance whether obviously or not (Kiesling, 2009). In other words, it imbues all social interaction, all utterances we make, and each one sits on a point along a stancetaking cline of conscious to unconscious and on a separate point along a related cline of explicitly stated to implied, with no 'time outs' from it (Du Bois and Kärkkäinen, 2012). It is an *activity*, signalled through diverse modalities, including facial expression, bodily positioning & movement, intonation and gaze (Lempert, 2009). Another way of putting it is to say that stancetaking manifests at all levels of linguistic production and communication and affects all meaning-making (Jaworski and Thurlow, 2009). What, then is meant by a stance? And what does 'taking' one entail and imply?

In this case, I will apply Kiesling's triadic model of stancetaking, which has been inspired by Du Bois's stance triangle (Kiesling, 2018, 2020, 2022) but with three fundamental changes. In Du Bois's model, a stance is given three parts. The three corners of the triangle are a 'stance object' plus a 'stance lead', and a 'stance follow' (both stance subjects) (Du Bois, 2007). The sides of the triangle represent the three dimensions:

(1) the stance lead's evaluation of the stance object;
(2) the stance follow's evaluation of the same stance object;
(3) the aligning or disaligning between the two evaluations.

However, Kiesling's model reconsiders the initiator(s) of the stancetaking process, which is a pivotal change (Englebretson, 2023). The role is recast via the addition of Goffman's tripartite notion of 'footing' (Goffman, 1981), splitting the stance subject into stance author, principal and animator. This move compels another modification whereby the three dimensions of the triangle are recast as evaluating (similar to Du Bois but not separating the stance subjects) and dis/aligning (as in Du Bois), but with the addition of *investing* in the creation of the stance (an investment that can be modulated). Another way to put it is that stance is treated as an umbrella term for positions that an interactional animator (in Goffman's sense) takes with respect to:

(1) entities referred to in the talk (a relationship of evaluation);
(2) other people or things involved in the interaction (a relationship of alignment);
(3) the talk itself (an affective relationship of investment).(Kiesling, 2020, 2022)

These changes lend the model additional explanatory power. It is the incorporation of Goffman's notion of footing that permits the addition of investment and affect to the mix due to the utility of these three separate types of footing. More fundamentally, Kiesling (2018, p. 198) states that 'stancetaking is a form of affective practice', by which he means (drawing on Wetherell, 2012) that affect and discourse are coupled and feed back to one another as we participate in stancetaking processes. That is, in the process of stancetaking the speakers speak, sign, gesture or write (animate) a stance that they might or might not have composed (authored), and for which they might or might not be the holder/taker of responsibility (principal). By adjusting these footings, the speaker can indicate affect via the levels of investment in the stancetaking underway, a modulation in 'affective context' or *tone* (Kiesling, 2018). For instance, with the doctors I interviewed, at times they are animating an institutional stance bid in which they invest to some extent because of their profession. However, they might or might not take full responsibility for it (i.e., speak as principal or avoid doing so) and might show low or high investment via the emotional tone they strike during the stancetaking process. It is important to emphasise that because stancetaking is an activity and process that is achieved in communicative interaction, all three footings are often distributed between two or more participants who might co-author and/or co-animate stances, sharing, mitigating, or deflecting responsibility for their implications. It follows that stances are a creation, over two or more conversational moves, of the relationship between the speaker and the entities spoken about, including stance bids by individuals, but the stance does not reside in any single utterance (Kiesling, 2020). In this web of stance activities, great insight can be gained into what the drivers behind the clinicians' evaluative and affective positionings could be (e.g., personal conviction, professional standards, institutional alignments, etc.) and where opportunities for interventions could lie.

Stancetaking analysis here requires a split-audience design (Linell, 2009), arguably inherent to the giving of accounts in interviews, with one stance triangle operating at the level of the immediate interaction with the interviewer and the other operating at the level of a 'remote' audience (Englebretson, 2023). In this case, the remote audience is the parents and patients in the accounts, who serve as abstractions of a target community or 'generalized others' (Linell, 2009 cited in Englebretson, 2023). They can also be characterized as 'distal' stance objects and subjects (Lempert, 2009), evaluated in the here-and-now of the interview but absent from it.

It will become clear during analysis that the clinicians give accounts of doing stancetaking while undertaking their duties. They simultaneously do stancetaking in the interview room, evaluating bodies and subjects as stance objects to varying levels of investment in those stances. Generalized parents and patients are accounted for as aligning with or 'disaligning' from the evaluations being developed.

What Is This Type of Analysis in Practice?

So, the interactional sociolinguistic analysis here brings together analysis of *representation* in language use with analysis of *evaluation* in language use; that is, the meta level, a social process 'about' the form and substance of speech. The representations and evaluations in language are also indicative of stancetaking on bodies and subjects, stancetaking on how to talk about them and stancetaking on 'why' to do it that way (both logically and morally). The stances in turn point to ideologies, many of which are bound up in biopolitical apparatuses and range in salience from latent to blatant.

Analytical Procedures

(1) I identified three sections of the interview recordings in which accounts of talk about patients' bodies became the focus, signalled by the use of common body vocabulary (e.g., body, genitals, hormones) and more technical biology/biomedical terms (e.g., gonad, phenotype, syndrome). These sections were transcribed and subsequently examined more closely.
(2) I then realized categories for analysis in a data-driven manner, with various regulatory social structures being made relevant in the transcribed sections (e.g., gender/sex, class, dis/ability) either by direct mention of those terms or through less direct discursive references (e.g., talk about boys and girls, fertility, (ab)normality, education level).
(3) Soon I noticed that meanings were accruing to these various structures in the data, with parents' subjectivities (signalled by talk of questions, reactions, social traits, responsibilities) emerging as equally important to patients' bodies as recurring points of focus in the accounts.
(4) My identification of these points of focus and more-or-less direct references to regulatory biopolitical apparatuses led to me to realize that the interviewees' talk involves stancetaking on how to talk to patients/parents.

Links to biopolitical apparatuses and ideological commitments became more clearly identifiable and traceable through this stancetaking. For this reason, the above process was not strictly linear; rather, points 2, 3 and 4 were more cyclical and mutually influencing as later realizations about bodies, subjectivities, biopolitical apparatuses and stancetaking prompted a review and enrichment of earlier preliminary analyses. I will make this process visible in the analysis in Sections 5 and 6 as I demonstrate which exact discursive moves (implicit and explicit) indicate stancetaking activity at a micro-interactional level (i.e., modulated investments, dis/alignments and/or evaluations by authors, animators and principals), these stance creations pointing in turn to meso-level ideologies and, in turn again, to macro-level biopolitics in action.

4.3.3 Structure of the Analytical Sections

I have elected to separate the analysis into two subdivisions – one focusing primarily on how sex characteristics are being shaped in the clinicians' accounts (Section 5), and the other taking the focus of how human subjects are also being shaped (Section 6). Ultimately, the two are imbricated, but for the purposes of exposition, I will highlight one more than the other in each section. Both processes are being described within the overall context of patient-centred medicine within the biomedical industrial complex, a standpoint on clinician-patient relations that brings its own affordances and constraints in relation to (non)authority, expertise, interaction, responsibility, and, at times, abandonment (Pilnick, 2022, 2023). I will discuss this aspect of context when clearly relevant.

5 Crafting Bodies: Biopower, Gender and Intersex Variations

I extracted the data for this section from interviews with Dr Yip and Dr Law.

5.1 Dr Yip

The theme of biopolitical management of intersex people (i.e., biopower) emerges in Yip's account via three overlapping biopolitical apparatuses that are latent in the doctor's discourse to varying degrees (or sometimes even overt): gender, biological sex and ableism. These apparatuses are anchored to the clinician's stancetaking activities, which provide the micro-level interactional evidence of biopolitics in action and overarching ideologies. Dr Yip's series of stancetaking processes constructs intersex variations as unnatural and diseased. The birth of a child with such variations is held to be a very urgent crisis because Hong Kong parents pathologize the child, an emergency that can reliably be solved only by current genetic science. This branch of science is deemed well-equipped to inform parents whether to raise the child as a boy or a girl. Furthermore, surgery is seen as an option unlikely to be regretted.

Prior to the first extract below, we had been discussing with whom Dr Yip usually speaks about bodies with intersex variations besides colleagues. The doctor confirmed speaking to both parents and people with intersex variations themselves at different life stages or moments. This is because certain body 'conditions' (mentioned by Yip prior to the extract) are evident at birth, so initially in such cases only parents face explanations, and explanations to the individuals themselves are deferred. Other categories of intersex variation become evident only at puberty, so in those cases, people with those variations face initial explanations alongside family members.

In Extract 1, I asked a question to Dr Yip during the English portion of the interview. As an interviewer, I yielded to Dr Yip's disorder-oriented framing; that is, I spoke in terms of medical 'conditions' (line 1), a word that signifies medical problems. Although it is possible to speak of benign shapes and structures in a conversation about bodies with intersex variations, the doctor had put those somatic formations under a disorder umbrella (i.e., DSD). I acquiesced at the time to elicit further explanation of how Dr Yip speaks to parents, specifically.

Extract 1 (Dr Yip)
(1) **BRIAN:** *[in English] So it seems like you've encountered quite a number*
(2) *of conditions that fit under the umbrella of Disorder of Sex Development,*
(3) *most of them would you say, of all the conditions that fit under the*
(4) *umbrella at some time you speak to the parents of children with those*
(5) *conditions?*
(6) **YIP:** *[in English] Yes, I always need to speak to them. Actually, for each of*
(7) *this case, we talk to them sequentially and continuously, because it's*
(8) *different, for example, before birth, the consideration, what they need to*
(9) *consider for the preparation, what will happen, or even they need to*
(10) *prepare that the sex of the baby cannot be determined at time of birth.*
(11) *This is quite a social emergency I would say because usually the*
(12) *parents ... while their relative would ask "Oh, have you given birth to a*
(13) *boy or girl?" And it's very embarrassing that they can't answer. So these*
(14) *are what they need to explain before birth. And after birth, we see them*
(15) *again, then we need to introduce to them how we assess the genitalia,*
(16) *what is the problem of the genitalia, and also any genetic tests that can*
(17) *help us to determine whether the baby should be raised as a boy or a girl.*

In line 11, Dr Yip explicitly uses the term 'social emergency' to characterize the inability to assign male or female at birth, initiating a stancetaking process in which intersex variations are evaluated negatively. In doing so the doctor animates a stance common in biomedicine internationally, namely that the birth of a baby with intersex variations is a crisis. This stance has long been identified as problematic, suggestive of assumptions (often baseless) about family members' reactions to bodies with intersex variations (Holmes, 2008; Jones, 2017). Just as importantly, it creates a sense of justification for medically unnecessary surgeries (Davis and Murphy, 2013). What, then, is the assumption being made in this case? In line 13, Dr Yip speaks of parents being unable to respond with a clear, obvious answer to the implied question behind the boy-girl query – that is, how their baby slots neatly into binary gender and sex. It is important to pursue why it should immediately escalate to an 'emergency' because at the root of this stance lies ableism, a bias and biopolitical apparatus that pervades much of medicine (Lundberg and Chen, 2024), but does not always generate neonatal emergencies. Yip is the animator of this pre-existing widespread stance, as observed, but animates it at a high level of investment (line 11 – *quite* a social emergency) and also acts as the principal (line 9 – *I would say*). In other words, although an animator and not the original author of this stance, Yip sets a stancetaking tone of extra urgency and manifestly takes responsibility for this stance bid.

What emerges from the discourse in Dr Yip's account is a sense that this 'social emergency' is being driven by an assumption that being able-bodied in all ways is the only desirable human form (Inckle, 2015) and it is an emergency because under an ableist lens, the child is 'lacking in the threshold level of ability that makes someone fully human' to those around them (Canagarajah, 2023, p. 5). Continuing the stance creation process, in line 13, Dr Yip frames as '*very embarrassing*' the prospect that parents might need to explain that their child's innate sex characteristics do not fit the compulsory dyad. Unpacking this 'emergency of embarrassment' stancetaking process, one might reasonably query why embarrassment should be the assumed response. Poorly primed parents might well find themselves underprepared and even frustrated by what had previously been, to them, an inconceivable outcome (Zeiler and Wickström, 2009). But it seems taken for granted here that most parents would be embarrassed about that child's body at the level of a 'social emergency'. Dr Yip thus aligns with an ideology of fused bioregulatory ableism and gendering in which a body with non-binary sex characteristics is a 'problem' (line 16) that cannot be left alone. The emergency framing and its accompanying discourses of embarrassment further bolster the doctor's high investment in the stance, which has an emotional impact that creates an 'affective context' or *tone* (Kiesling, 2018) for the reported consultation. The tone of urgency infuses the whole process.

Emergencies generate fear and anxiety and so demand action (Scarry, 2011; Davis and Murphy, 2013), and the doctor alludes to that response in lines 11–14. This focus on finding the genetic answer to the baby's boy/girl status is about trying to work out how to advise the parents about the 'sex of rearing' of the baby, regardless of whether surgery is to be postponed or done immediately. Effort is made to use physical evidence of the baby's fetal development to make this decision, initiating another stancetaking process in which current science is positively evaluated as capable of reliable answers to this question, delivered in a matter-of-fact tone (lines 16–17 – *genetic tests that can help us*). Wittingly or not, the doctor is animating a stance that was placed in wide circulation among clinicians in the divisive and contentious 'Chicago Consensus' statement (Hughes et al., 2006) in which sex was deemed to reside at the genetic level, awaiting recognition. This cause-finding framing conceals that in fact the reason is often a mystery (see Dr Law's account in Extract 3 below). Dr Yip implies that girlishness and boyishness (i.e., gender) can be predicted by effectively drilling down to the DNA (i.e., biological sex). There is in fact no conclusive evidence for this assertion (Rosario, 2009; Fausto-Sterling, 2012; Lee et al., 2016; Hutton, 2019). But the doctor's stancetaking places it as fact that gender is dependent on biological sex, lending weight to the idea that sexual difference is also a biopolitical apparatus (see Section 1). This process becomes clearer in the next extract as it also becomes mingled with another stancetaking process around Hong Kong culture. This extract picks up directly from the previous one in the middle of an extended turn taken by Dr Yip.

Extract 2 (Dr Yip cont'd)
(18) *There are limitations in sex assignment in some of the cases, that is, under*
(19) *the umbrella of DSD, some of them sex assignment is very straightforward,*
(20) *because we know the disease, know the natural history of the disease, so*
(21) *we know that this should be a girl or this should be a boy. But there are*
(22) *some cases within the DSD spectrum that being a girl or being a boy is not a*
(23) *perfect answer, they need to think about the pros and cons of being boy or a*
(24) *girl, or it's less likely in Hong Kong, but in some other places they want to*
(25) *keep the baby unisex for more longer time. Although I haven't come across*
(26) *this in Hong Kong, I think in Hong Kong context most of the parents would*
(27) *prefer to assign at least one sex to the baby, and even though they know that*
(28) *there is a small chance that the baby want to revert it when they grow older,*
(29) *but they want to give a certain sex as soon as possible.*

Continuing uninterrupted (Extract 2), the doctor then refers to some children with intersex variations for whom '*sex assignment is very straightforward*' (line 19). Their bodies are essentialized as either male or female via Dr Yip's stance that their 'disease' is deemed to have deviated their bodies from the original 'natural' pathway, so we see biopower at work as the doctor's stance bid animates this common stance from biomedicine, negatively evaluating these variations in *innate* sex characteristics as diseased bodies by *denaturalizing* them. This stancetaking shows high investment by Dr Yip, evidenced by the term *disease*, which is eminently pathologizing (see Table 1 below), creating a sober tone in the interview. This process serves to pathologize, opening intersex variations up to biopolitical management as bodies in need of correction (i.e., it 'justifies' surgery under the two-sex model). There is no consideration given, here, to the possibility that their bodies need not be negatively evaluated and pathologized. Along the way, in lines 24–29, Yip begins weaving in another stancetaking process, authoring and taking personal responsibility for a stance (i.e., *I think*) that Hong Kong culture propels parents to settle swiftly on an assigned sex. This stance is partly achieved by diminishing (and so negatively evaluating) the notion that sex assignment should wait, projecting it onto '*some other places*' (line 24) and so othering its advocates. The stance is taken that it is not the Hong Kong way.

Whether they 'should' be reared as a boy or girl and probably '*in Hong Kong*' (lines 24–25) have associated surgeries, is not based on phenotype (i.e., body appearance) in Dr Yip's account but another, perhaps genetic, measure, indicating stancetaking in which science is positively evaluated as knowing definitively how to determine sex of rearing reliably. Gender is acting as a regulatory structure in this case because (in the doctor's discourse) it is the parents' urge for a binary-*gendered* child (i.e., either a boy or a girl) that seems to drive binary *sex* assignment and the pathologization of the child's intersex variations of innate sex characteristics. What are the relations of biopower underlying gender's role in bioregulation here? In the doctor's interview discourse, the parents have no sense that they could raise the baby as a boy, for instance, and leave his genitals alone, and provide social support.

Table 1 Available Chinese malady terms

Character	Jyutping (Cantonese 'pinyin')	English equivalent	Literal translation
疾病	zat^6 beng^6 (tone low level)	*Disease/illness*	*Disease*
障礙	zoeng^3 ngoi^6 (tone mid, low)	*Disorder*	*Obstacle*
小病	siu^2 beng^6 (tone mid rising, low)	*Ailment*	*Minor illness*
病痛	beng^6 tung^3 (tone low, mid)	*Sickness*	*Suffering, indisposition*
狀態	zong^6 taai^3 (tone low, mid)	*Condition*	*Status*

Followers of this advice are othered, and Hong Kong culture is constructed as obdurate to this alternative. The doctor could offer a parent options by pointing out this non-surgery option, but Dr Yip leaves it out of the account. Such an omission would fit with a well-documented international trend in which parents of intersex-bodied children are offered 'surgery or nothing' in just such a problematic manner (Roen, 2019). There are ableist underpinnings to this account of a patient-centred medicine encounter, for we see yet again that parents might not truly be presented with options – rather, the course of action is tacitly laid out. The embodiment of their child is 'catastrophised' by the doctor's stancetaking in this account of a consultation, which is ableist and a product of biopower.

In a second scenario (still Extract 2, lines 22–29), *uncertainty* emerges, serving as what Pilnick and Zayts, in their conversation analysis of antenatal screening counselling sessions, have described as ' . . . an issue to talk with; an interactional resource that can be drawn on to support quite different interpretations' (Pilnick and Zayts, 2014, p. 197). Here it is drawn on as a stancetaking investment mitigation strategy. In line 28, Dr Yip uses the term '*a small chance*', evaluating as unlikely (yet possible) the notion that the child might later want to revert the assigned sex. Yip's stancetaking process thus suggests that sex assignment is an uncertain pathway and the child (and parent) could later regret the sexual assignment, but the doctor asserts low investment in this evaluation by minimizing regret's probability and so minimizing risk. There is again an ideology at work by which surgery is portrayed optimistically as an option via this tone. This stancetaking process is also seen in Timmermans et al. (2018), whereby clinicians, even if cautioning against haste, evaluate sex assignment optimistically in more or less direct ways. In Dr Yip's account, parents are the ones positioned as driving this decision of 'surgery or not' (i.e., it is presented as what Hong Kong parents want in line 27, again communicating a low investment in the animation of this stance on Yip's part). This stancetaking process is evidence of an ideology that positions Hong Kong parents as the ones who pathologize these children. Meanwhile this hypothetical parent is being asked to engage in biopolitical management, imposing control on their own child's body yet influenced by a clinician's implied optimism that there is only a very '*small chance*' that surgery would be regretted. It is a cogent example of how intersex embodiments cannot be completely separated from parent subjectivity formation (the focus of Section 6).

Looking at it from another angle, the doctor's account leverages uncertainty via mixed messaging. The child's body in this introduced scenario seems to elude capture by the binary gender apparatus (lines 23–24 – '*being a girl or being a boy is not a perfect answer*'), but control is exercised anyway, with parents positioned as the controllers. Yet, it is important to ask whether the doctor is abdicating responsibility (not just relinquishing authority) as part of 'patient-centred care' (Liao, 2022; Roen et al., 2023). Could uncertainty be deployed here to boost the doctor's influence in the shared decision-making of a patient-centred care scenario with parents as surrogate decision makers? Or is it rather a deployment of a clinician's perceived 'expertise' to say to parents that there is a '*small chance*' the child might be unhappy with the gender assignment later in life? If that were the case, then speaking up on the topic might be enforced by interactional demands of clinician-patient interaction (Pilnick, 2022), where biomedical professionals are expected to contribute expertise even if relinquishing authority. They are forced in their role to navigate interactionally between competing moral norms about directiveness versus non-directiveness.

5.2 Discussion (Dr Yip)

The trouble with this last assessment would be that there is really no reliable evidence that the chance of regret is in fact 'small'; there is a shortage of reliable research on long-term effects of childhood sex assignment surgeries (Baratz and Feder, 2015; Liao et al., 2019; Balocchi and Kehrer, 2020; Muschialli et al., 2024), so meaningful expertise is stretched thin with this topic. Rather, clinicians' faith in childhood surgeries as a solution amounts to 'vague and evaluative beliefs' by which silence from former patients is said to signal satisfaction with their surgical assignment (Carpenter, 2018, p. 459). Readily available and mounting testimony from those whom childhood surgery has harmed has largely been dismissed by medical practitioners (Carpenter, 2016, 2024), who ironically lack evidence for their own testimony, effectively a hackneyed reanimation of the Nixonian anachronism 'the silent majority speaking'. The most recent study to attempt such an investigation found that a great many adults expressed dissatisfaction with the effects of their childhood surgery (Köhler et al., 2012). It has been difficult to conduct these follow-up studies because stigma, trauma and disaffection keep people silent (King, 2022a; Carpenter, Kraus and Earp, 2024), or they 'go missing' from biomedical networks as an act of resistance (Malatino, 2019), or even more basically, lack awareness because of a lack of information arising from the regime of secrecy that has tended to be encouraged in biomedical circles (Karkazis, 2008). To put it plainly, it seems expertise and authority are both thin in this tale.

At the root of Yip's stancetaking sequence lies ableism via the 'catastrophizing' of non-malignant bodily variations, but binary gender and biological sex are entangled together and fused with this ableism. In this formulation, there are only boys and girls (gender), so there must only be boy genes and girl genes.

Biological sex sets the agenda via binary genetics, we are told. And so it goes round. In fact, sex is on a spectrum in biological science and not strictly about genes (Professor of Paediatric Endocrinology John Achermann, quoted in Ainsworth, 2015), but binary gender dictates the response to a non-binary body. It is regulatory. As Celeste Orr has explored, biological sex is constructed as a 'compulsory dyad' (2023) that she positions as itself an iteration of 'compulsory ablebodiedness' (McRuer, 2006; Inckle, 2015). That is, there is a cultural mandate that people cannot have intersex variations and must embody and reaffirm the male/female biological sex dyad (Orr, 2023), a manifestation of the biological sex apparatus, which is itself enforced as binary, but further boosted by its entanglement with the binary gender apparatus (Clune-Taylor, 2020).

By existing outside the dyad, intersex variations sit outside of compulsory ablebodiedness and so are lent more easily to stances that evoke a sense of social emergency. The social emergency mentality can be traced to eugenics movements of the first half of the twentieth century. Feminist philosopher McWhorter (2010, p. 56) quotes Lee Dice, director of the University of Michigan's genetic counselling centre, who suggested in 1952 that parents could be 'guided', within the precepts of patient-centred medicine it seems, to 'decide for themselves' that a child's birth would be a 'calamity' for them and a burden on their community (Dice, 1952, p. 12). Extending it further, McWhorter insightfully points out that with the 'right' policies and social expectations, such births could be *made* to be calamitous for mothers and fathers increasingly isolated in suburban nuclear family units. It can be no mere coincidence that Dice made these statements at the precise time that John Money was publishing his theories about 'emergency' surgeries on intersex babies to secure their position in the nuclear family (Repo, 2016; Malatino, 2019). This scenario has been framed variously as 'flexible eugenics' (Mills, 2018) and as 'eugenics from below' (Loveland, 2017). That is, eugenics has been passed to the individual parent, who engages in biopolitical management via a 'biotechnological apparatus of choice' (Mills, 2018, p. 154), and so the enactment of freedom, of control (Pilnick, 2022), is a site for biopolitical management. Loveland (2017) also explores this regime in detail.

Strict human dimorphism is a zombie fact that here 'claws' its way in the guise of 'biological sex' (an elusive notion, yet a powerful apparatus) to the rescue of the regulatory apparatus of binary gender:

> [Individuals with intersex features] are stigmatized and traumatized because western biomedicine and hegemonic legal and social institutions are *deeply invested in maintaining the ideologies of sexual dimorphism and binary gender (my emphasis)* (Rubin, 2017, pp. 92–93).

So, we see that the apparatuses of gender and sex difference are mutually determinative of one another in this case. It is of course the binary version of gender, not a more expansive version, but it is in biopolitics and bioregulation that binary gender remains dominant because its absence might in turn unravel the apparatus of binary sex difference. Without the two propping each other up, each is highly vulnerable.

As feminist philosopher Nancy Tuana has emphasized, we must speak of ignorance production as much as knowledge production in order to understand why scientifically unsound notions can live on among people who should know better:

> Ignorance – far from being a simple, innocent lack of knowledge – is a complex phenomenon that like knowledge, is interrelated with power; for example, ignorance is frequently constructed, and it is linked to issues of cognitive authority, trust, doubt, silencing, etc. (Tuana, 2004, p. 226).

The silencing referred to by Tuana is often also the result of deliberate or inadvertent neglect of topics, which inevitably arise out of uncertainty, implicit and explicit bias, and patterns of unconscious 'not noticing'. The analyses in Section 5 have provided numerous examples of these phenomena and helped to illuminate how the shaping of intersex variations takes place in a structuring web of biopower in healthcare communication that pathologizes those characteristics relentlessly.

In the next selected interview, Dr Law does not engage in the emergency-invoking stancetaking evident in Dr Yip's account, but uncertainty and pathologization remain in evidence. As the account unfolds, parents are ostensibly offered options once again, but it again becomes questionable whether these choices are offered up in such a way that achieves non-directiveness.

5.3 Dr Law

Dr Law's stancetaking, although procedurally distinct from Dr Yip's, still ends up reinforcing the biopolitical fusion of ableism, sex and gender. Intersex traits are pathologized by Chinese parents in their discourse, creating urgency and emotional distress at birth that must then be managed. While Law diminishes the necessity of surgery, emphasizing gender of rearing as an alternative source of control for parents, in the end this stancetaking is seen to offer only limited liberation. Predictions of the child's future gender identity are said to rely on observing others with similar characteristics, yet ultimately, Law presumes these feelings are determined by the body. Biological sex thus operates as the regulating apparatus, constraining gender's possibilities and narrowing agency.

Prior to Extract 3 (below), the Cantonese portion of the interview had just commenced as Interviewer 2 took over, and the discussion had turned to the tendency for parents to look up terms on the internet after the initial consultation about their child's innate sex characteristics. Dr Law had suggested that regardless of whether or not they were provided with medical terms, people would invariably turn to the Internet for more information. For this reason, the doctor believed it best to furnish them with the technical biomedical terms of the child's diagnosis in the hope parents would find 'accurate' information while searching. As Dr Law revisits in lines 3–6, any confusion or misunderstanding could be sorted out at the follow-up consultation(s). Interviewer 2 then questions the use of technical language with parents in such a way (lines 1 and 2).

Extract 3 (Dr Law)
(1) **INTERVIEWER 2:** *But wouldn't they have a lot of follow-up questions,*
(2) *since these terms just introduced are very complicated words?*
(3) **LAW:** *Yes, it's very reasonable to have questions, because for example we*
(4) *would introduce to them a more broader umbrella term, then afterwards*
(5) *they will of course have a lot of questions. And usually, we wouldn't only*
(6) *have one session, there will be ongoing sessions, explaining and*
(7) *revisiting the (6) questions etc . . .*
(8) **INTERVIEWER 2:** *What type of the questions would they ask?*
(9) **LAW:** *Usually they would first ask "What is this illness? Why did it occur?"*
(10) *But really, most of the cases are very difficult to explain for sure why it*
(11) *occurs, that's just what is. Also, other questions directed to me are . . . well*
(12) *because usually I will be consulting them together with a paediatrician, who*
(13) *are responsible for their follow up, whether or not if medicine or drug is*
(14) *required to prescribe to the patient. And for me it's about whether or not the*
(15) *patient needs surgery, or when is the surgery needed, so yeah these are the*
(16) *questions that I usually encounter.*
(17) **INTERVIEWER 2:** *How about the parents? Are any of them opposed to*
(18) *surgeries?*
(19) **LAW:** *Well . . . umm . . . opposing, not really. But yeah like we discussed,*
(20) *I understand that, especially in article papers, there is some expressed*
(21) *opinions that they do not want to have the surgery. But actually, in contrast,*
(22) *for those with a strong Chinese culture mindset, they actually really want*
(23) *the gender to be assigned. And we think it is possible, but also we would*
(24) *educate the parents that you can assign a gender to the child, but actually*
(25) *surgery is not required for the kid to be assigned a gender. You can still raise*
(26) *the kid by following a specific gender and supporting them that way. Also,*

Language, Gender and Biopolitics 39

(27) *even if you help the kid determine their gender, it doesn't mean that in future*
(28) *the kid will follow through with their gender assigned at birth, however we*
(29) *don't have U "unassigned" as a classification of sex in Hong Kong, we only*
(30) *have male or female, no matter what type of official documents, we*
(31) *currently do not have U. But at the hospital setting, we can temporarily*
(32) *declare a U for the baby, especially when we cannot determine the sex. So*
(33) *this means that the baby can of course change their gender anytime they*
(34) *want, including hospital and other official governmental systems.*

Interviewer 2 launches a stancetaking interaction in a bid that negatively evaluates technical language in this context as '*complicated*' and likely to trigger questions from parents (lines 1 and 2). Law aligns to this stance bid to a degree in lines 3–5, agreeing that questions are a '*reasonable*' response, but moderates this alignment by explaining that many steps are taken to manage the process of informing parents. In line 9 Dr Law then authors a stancetaking move in which parents' questions are negatively evaluated, as they are inclined to ask '*What is this illness? Why did it occur?*' So, there is an evaluation of parents (as generalized others) in which they are primarily concerned with what is 'wrong' with their child. That is, a stance is building in which parents are bound to have a pathologizing reaction.

Before digging more deeply into this stancetaking, it is necessary to note that the question of why their child's body occurred in an 'ill' form is framed as unanswerable. In line 11, Law says '*that's just what is*' in a markedly candid confession of biomedicine's limited understanding of intersex variations of innate sex characteristics. The effect is to disalign from the negative evaluation of intersex variations and from the pathologizing ascribed to the hypothetical parent (and child), saying they just need to accept the situation. This is very different from a stance creation in which the birth of a child with intersex variations is a psychosocial emergency (as seen in Dr Yip's account previously). Dr Law's interview stancetaking on the pathologizing mindset of parents is then further bolstered in lines 21–25 with reference to Chinese culture, saying that Chinese parents '*actually really want the gender to be assigned*' as part of a pro-surgery tendency. The use of '*actually really*' as a modifying adverbial creates disalignment from the assumption that parents will defer surgery and is an affective assertion of high investment in this stance, creating a tone of urgency around Chinese parents.

An ideology pixelates into view in which parents arrive with a powerfully pathologizing mindset because they are Chinese. However, this stancetaking sits awkwardly beside the information, provided by Dr Law prior to this extract, that parents are first given medicalized names for their child's physical formation and sent away to do their own research on biomedical terminology given to them by a clinician almost certainly clad in a white coat. Chinese or not, the pathologization has already tacitly taken place via seeds planted by Dr Law's initial use of medicalized language and by the hospital setting (see also Liao, 2022). The account then takes a turn (lines 23–25), with Dr Law self-positioning as using expertise to educate parents to the idea that you can assign a gender without resorting to surgery. Here, stancetaking continues to evaluate parents as pathologizers (i.e., they need educating), but now there is an option on offer besides doing surgery or doing nothing; that is, they can have control of their child's well-being via the gender of rearing.

In this way, gender comes into play in Dr Law's account of educating parents, but not in its coercive biopolitical form. In lines 23–34, gender is made relevant, and we see that gender is separated from the body in this case (lines 24–25 – *you can assign a gender to the child but actually surgery is not required*). Parents can be '*educated*' to realize that surgery is *not* required for the child to live as the assigned gender. Concurrent with this stancetaking about parents as a remote audience in the account, which has been the analytical focus so far, is a process of stancetaking in the interview context whereby gender is evaluated positively as having *emancipatory* capacities because it allows the child's pathologized body to escape surgical management. Far from being captured by gender or eluding it, the child is liberated by it in this account because the child later gains autonomy (line 27 '*You can help the kid determine their gender*' but '*it doesn't mean that in future the kid will follow through*'). Dr Law is animating a stance bid, originally authored among intersex rights activists (Chase, 2003), that points to an ideology in which their anatomy is not their destiny, and in fact their anatomy has *little to do with* the viability and livability of their life. Importantly, parents are still enacting control if they forego surgery, '*following a specific gender and supporting*' their child (line 26), but their management is seen to be social rather than surgical.

But in this realm of surrogate-led patient-centred medicine, how realistically can we expect that this non-surgery option might be chosen? In this account, Dr Law professes relinquishing authority to parents in line with patient-centred medicine's shared decision-making model in paediatrics, and there has not been a withdrawal of expertise resulting in abandonment as too often happens (Roen et al., 2023). Yet in the face of the overriding pathologization of medical terminology and medical surroundings, are parents still being beguiled and manoeuvred? Continuing an extended turn at talk, Law goes on to further explain how the gender of rearing is settled upon.

> Extract 4 (Dr Law cont'd)
> (35) *But how can we tell a baby about if they are going to be a boy or girl and how*
> (36) *do they make sense of what they want in the future, you might wonder. For*
> (37) *this, we would base on the individual condition of the patient, following past*
> (38) *cases as example to see what the patients will end up choosing and*
> (39) *agreeing with their sex. For example, CAH,[3] most patients would think that*
> (40) *they are female, but of course we know not all them would have the same*
> (41) *understanding. A more severe case like hypospadias, they would tend to*
> (42) *agree upon the fact that they are male. Of course, these are not absolute,*
> (43) *but it could have an effect to the parents on how they will raise the kid.*
> (44) *Secondly, we also have cases that are in the middle, undetermined, so we*
> (45) *would look at the test results on the testosterone level, how much it*
> (46) *presents. This is because through understanding retrospectively from*
> (47) *previous cases, if the child would have more influence from the*
> (48) *testosterone level, there is high likeliness of them accepting themselves to*
> (49) *be male. But this is only for this one specific case. Others like for example*
> (50) *AIS,[4] we wouldn't explain them the same logic. For cases like complete AIS,*
> (51) *the patients will mostly identify themselves as female. So we will go through*
> (52) *related cases and scenarios to kind of inform the parents and make project*
> (53) *what is the likelihood of sex that the child will identify in the future.*

In this extract, advising the parents how to decide the gender of rearing is presented as being based on what '*most patients*' with the same diagnosis tend to *feel*, which animates stancetaking originally authored by intersex patient advocates, expressly, 'This guess should be based upon the available data – that is, what we know about gender identity outcomes in other patients with a similar diagnosis and presentation' (Chase, 2003, p. 241). Stancetaking is thus underway in the interview context concerning the degree to which the assessments of people with intersex variations themselves, that is, what we know about outcomes, have reliably been surveyed. That is, Law is building a stance with a positive evaluation of the extent to which these preferences have been confirmed as opposed to just assumed because 'silent majorities speak' (as with Dr Yip, Extract 2). In lines 39–42, '*most*' of those classified in the somatic category of CAH are said to identify as female, and those categorized in the hypospadias category '*would tend to agree*' they are men. Law strikes a moderate tone by signalling a mitigated investment in the developing stance by conceding (line 40) that '*not all*' would understand

---

[3] Congenital Adrenal Hyperplasia. [4] Androgen Insensitivity Syndrome.

themselves that way and (line 41) saying they '*tend*' to agree. Again, a stance is forming that suggests anatomy is not *necessarily* destiny and predicting gender identity is an imprecise practice, but this assessment requires closer scrutiny.

As previously observed, the focus in the doctor's account remains on how the people are purported to *feel* rather than on genetic makeup or body formations. Gender as a system of power is manifest here through a sense that gender is not reliably determined by sex. However, importantly, it is still tethered to bodies and pathologization because their *diagnosis* is used to shape the guidance. In Extract 5, the doctor continues the same extended turn at talk, continuing stancetaking activity around the idea that gender identity is predictable from bodies. However, this stancetaking process is imbricated with other developing stances.

Extract 5 (Dr Law cont'd)
(54) *But we will stress to the parent that they shouldn't feel pressured about the*
(55) *fact that they need to fill in an exact information on the birth certificate to*
(56) *make this particular decision. Another thing is, even if they made the wrong*
(57) *decision, they could make changes later on. And thirdly, I will emphasize*
(58) *that this is not the parents' fault that their kid has these condition. I will*
(59) *explain to them that it is like other illness like for example diabetes and*
(60) *hypertension, it's the same, it's an illness, some people are born with it. You*
(61) *just need accept that you have the illness, and willing to treat it and live with*
(62) *it, and live in a relatively normal social setting, then you would be fine. Do*
(63) *not define yourself using the illness condition, first you need to accept it and*
(64) *then you can think about how to deal with it later. As for treatment like*
(65) *surgery, the discussion will eventually come in the follow-up session, as*
(66) *course of treatment. I will very clearly tell the parents that they do not need*
(67) *to decide immediately, if there is no emergency that requires surgery. I think*
(68) *it's more important to emphasize and focus on the parents understanding of*
(69) *the conditions of their child, rather than discuss surgery options at that*
(70) *moment.*

In lines 54–57, Law continues to strike a tone of appeasement by signalling a middling to low investment in the developing stance that suggests bodies predict gender identities. The doctor claims to tell parents that, even though the birth certificate requires a recorded sex at birth, it would be possible to correct it later if the '*wrong*' gender identity were assigned. Law then returns to the stancetaking process around the Chinese parent, which is imbricated with stancetaking on innate sex characteristics. There is mounting tension between these two processes as Law speaks of intersex variations as a non-emergency, and no one's fault, yet still framing these children's bodies as diseased and ill – abnormal – something requiring treatment. In line 58, the Chinese parent is evaluated as *likely* to be feeling at '*fault*' for their child's body. The word *fault* has negative prosody and implies guilty feelings, and so continues to build the stancetaking begun in Extract 3 via which Chinese parents are ultimately positioned as pathologizers requiring education. Fault implies feelings of wrongdoing, so this stancetaking on Chinese parents could point to discourses around the self in Confucian heritage societies. In such discourses, relationships with others should ideally contribute to social welfare and harmony, but the birth of a child with a developmental 'abnormality' is perceived to disrupt this contribution (Lu, 2008) and can lead to social discrimination against the family (Huang et al., 2020). It is difficult from this account to be certain about the relevance of these alleged ethnic practices, however, for it is also possible that guilt can arise in parents of any cultural background when saddled with making a momentous and uncertain choice on behalf of their baby. In any case, Dr Law is talking about (line 58) the need to assuage feelings of guilt, where parents are assured that they are not at fault. The doctor's account then weaves in some more stancetaking on intersex variations, several times using the Cantonese term zat^6 beng^6 (low tone), which means *disease/illness* (lines 59, 60 and 61). This term is maximally pathologizing (see Table 5.1, Extract 2 section).

5.4 Discussion (Dr Law)

As discussed in the analysis of Dr Yip's account, robust follow-up research on these questions about how those with intersex variations identify is lacking. Yet, indisputably, a decision does have to be made about how to gender the child (by parents), and in this account, Dr Law is telling how they respond in a non-directive (i.e., patient-centred) way to parents who ask the doctor how to make this monumental decision on behalf of a baby. As Pilnick (2022, 2023) points out in her analysis of clinician-patient interactions, there are good *interactional* reasons for providing parents with some guidance despite the imperative (in the patient-centred model) of not being directive. It is normal in medical consultations for news to be followed by elaboration of a diagnosis and a proposal of alternative forms of action (Pilnick, 2022). So, to respond with reticence to a parent's request for assistance, neglecting to present some kind of expert knowledge, would be very much a 'dispreferred response' in this context (to borrow the terminology of Conversation Analysis). In the account, Dr Law navigates the patient-centred medicine imperative by framing guidance as information-providing rather than advising, but there is still an undercurrent of advice. As Pilnick (2022, p. 67) argues, ' ... it is, in practice, incredibly difficult to produce a truly neutral utterance', and so non-directiveness is nigh on unachievable in interaction.

Sequence can affect how options are heard, so choices offered might not feel like choices, and if the clinician succeeds in giving a sense of choice, they hand over a potentially unwanted *burden* of choice and its accompanying guilt, which is amplified when making decisions on behalf of another (Pilnick, 2022). In the case of Law's account, a stance is built in which anatomy is not *necessarily* destiny and predicting gender identity from bodies is an imprecise practice, and so gender of rearing can provide the solution to giving the child a liveable life without infant surgery. But ultimately a stance is taken that suggests the patient's body shapes their feelings about gender in most cases, thus a stance that contributes to curtailing the liberatory framing of gender. That is, ideologically speaking, anatomy is still *indirectly* destiny in this account.

Despite a markedly different stancetaking process from Dr Yip, Dr Law's series of stancetaking processes is still ultimately evidence of a fusing of ableism, sex and gender in biopolitics. Intersex variations are framed as diseased and as strongly pathologized via Chinese parents, creating urgency at a child's birth and guilt and anxiety about the child's well-being. But surgery is evaluated as unnecessary in this stancetaking, with gender of rearing providing control instead, suggesting that gender as a lived reality can be liberating (apparently quite a departure from Yip's stancetaking). Deciding future gender identity in Law's case is imprecise but aided by observation of how others with similar sex characteristics have felt. But at the end of the day, the stance suggests that those feelings are determined by their body. This means that biological sex is the apparatus that regulates gender, so gender's potential is curtailed. And so we see the biopolitical apparatus of 'biological sex' holding sway, pathologizing these characteristics and limiting the choices on offer once again. I will next turn my attention to the creation of affected subjects, which provides insight into where agency in the face of biopower may lie.

6 Crafting Subjects: Biopower, Gender and the Good Parent

To quote intersex studies pioneer Morgan Holmes, 'Autonomy may always be provisional, but to deny some their bodily integrity – as with intersexed children – on the grounds that autonomy is only provisional at best is to continue to divide the world into groups of people who are more and less deserving, with some more able to exercise their provisional autonomy than others' (Holmes, 2008, p. 179). Because parents get directly recruited into the biopolitical positioning of their children with intersex variations as less deserving of provisional autonomy, it is essential to see how their own subject formation is crafted in the process.

The data for this second analysis section has been extracted from interviews with Dr Fung, Dr Ngai and Dr Au. The focus in this section shifts more squarely onto accounts of the biopolitical management of parents – that is, the crafting of parents into biopolitical managers of their children in indirect and direct ways. In the previous section, where the focus of analysis was the crafting of bodies with intersex variations, there were moments when this shaping of the 'good parent' had already come into view because the two processes are not fully separate. That is, shaping parents as biopolitical managers entails clinicians creating stances on intersex variations, and this stancetaking precipitates related perceptions of special management that the child will need. But a full exploration of this shaping of parent perception requires moving beyond bodies into subjecthood.

As outlined in Section 1, to understand the biopolitical management of bodies with intersex variations one must understand the role that pathologizing such bodies has played in the racial politics of European colonialism and its quest to stamp out abnormality, especially to conceal it among white people (King, 2023a). 'Biological sex' was, from its foundational moments, racialized into differing categories, with Black people perceived as the least sexually dimorphic and white people the most sexually dimorphic. This notion fed into the whiteness of surgical correction to maintain white supremacy (Meyers, 2022). That is, white babies whose bodies did not fit a strict sexual dimorphism were 'fixed' to maintain the fiction that white people were more sexually dimorphic, and hence displaying a superior 'orderly homogeneity'. It is a biopolitics of race, sex and gender, and its colonialist logics live on in our (unwitting) current practices, as Foucault realized. In the narrative of nineteenth century 'hermaphrodite' Herculine Barbin, Foucault identifies a significant shift in the European approach to sex. By the end of the nineteenth century, it became mandatory for everyone to identify with a specific sex, either male or female; the concept of being both or a combination was not accepted while it had previously enjoyed some tolerance despite the pathologization outlined here (Foucault, 1980). As Repo (2014, p. 86) has said, ' ... the biopolitical order sought to trap and order [Barbin] as a sexed human being'. This legacy in turn influenced John Money and others, leading to the dominant programme of managing the perceptions of child patients through surgery and rearing, but importantly also managing the perceptions of their parents.

Crafting perceiving parent subjects is a key aspect of biopolitical management, recruiting them into the management of their child's body but with certain ratified perceptions. It is important to acknowledge that the 'steering' of parent perceptions by clinicians is not inherently wrong or something that should be discouraged by its very nature; it is the nature of the ratified perceptions that matters. This crafting potentially has both emancipatory and regulatory aspects when the awaited result is liveable lives for people with intersex variations.

Indeed, the next interviewee, Dr Fung, seems to speak of shaping a perception in parents that the lives of child and parent *are* both viable and liveable from the beginning, and gender is the linchpin of this perception. This stancetaking can be seen as emancipatory, yet testimony has shown that other more regulatory perceptions have been, and still are, propagated among parents via the same process. The question is, does infant surgery get woven into the framing of a life as more liveable? Or less so?

6.1 Dr Fung

Dr Fung's stancetaking on communication with parents of children with intersex variations orients towards managing language carefully to encourage parental participation in care without triggering stigma. By giving an account of strategically using English biomedical terms rather than their Cantonese equivalents, Fung builds a stance by which the use of Cantonese is negatively evaluated because it alarms parents by indexing negative connotations attached to Cantonese medical vocabulary. Fung's stancetaking negatively evaluates Chinese parents, portraying them as needing guidance to move away from pathologizing views of intersex variations, particularly emphasizing education as a factor gauging their receptivity. Ultimately, Fung's discourse reveals efforts to manage both linguistic and ideological boundaries, encouraging parents to act as biopolitical managers aligned with modern biomedical perspectives rather than traditional cultural interpretations.

Prior to Extract 6, I had followed the established routine of opening the interview in English. Following my prompt about speaking to different audiences, Dr Fung had said, unsurprisingly, that speaking to a child directly about their intersex variations required a very different approach from that used when speaking to parents. Description and hand-drawn images were said to be relied on heavily, and of course vocabulary had to be graded to their level. They spoke of the need to grade language to the level of a listener's knowledge base as one of the main challenges with talking about intersex variations outside of discussions with their colleagues. As we approached the transition of the interview into Cantonese with Interviewer 2, I asked about the use of the term DSD, and after Line 8 Interviewer 2 took over.

Extract 6 (Dr Fung)
(1) **BRIAN:** *[In English] How about the term "DSD"? Do you use this with*
(2) *children and parents or mostly your colleagues?*
(3) **FUNG:** *[In English] Most of the time, with parents, if you throw out the*
(4) *terms like Disorders of sex development, for ordinary Chinese families – I*
(5) *mean the Chinese families are not as traditional as before but if you talk*
(6) *about sex and stuff, they will feel more drawback. So, we don't want them to*
(7) *have this kind of impression at the very beginning. We want them to engage*
(8) *in the management of the kid, so we would try to explain to them in like "this*
(9) *situation is kind of a variant to the usual kind of presentation but not exactly*
(10) *very abnormal". Otherwise, they may not accept their kids as much.*
*** *(section omitted in which Interviewer 2 took over in Cantonese, revisiting speaking to kids)* ***
(27) **INTERVIEWER 2:** *[In Cantonese] Do you see a significant difference when*
(28) *you translate the message to different parents? Like some of them may be*
(29) *highly educated or . . . so.*
(30) **FUNG:** *[In Cantonese] Oh yes, very different. So, for more educated*
(31) *parents, the explanation feels much easier. At least, they can grasp the*
(32) *concepts like genetic male or female may not look completely like boys or*
(33) *girls, in a way that their sexual organs may or may not be like boys or girls.*
(34) *They can understand and accept this more easily. But, if you were to explain*
(35) *it to families of lower socio-economic class, they might just become fixated*
(36) *on asking "So is this a boy or a girl", instead of understanding what is*
(37) *happening in the back, so they're at a different level actually. Also,*
(38) *sometimes they cannot understand more complicated terms. So, we*
(39) *usually evaluate the level of acceptance of the family and decide on how*
(40) *many meetings to have with them. We'll still try to explain, but maybe in*
(41) *more sessions. But, the families are fixated on "oh, so is this a boy or a girl,*
(42) *does this affect fertility", and so. It becomes about being realistic – or what*
(43) *they think to be realistic needs.*

In my question (lines 1–2), as an interviewer, I made the first bid in a stancetaking process, negatively evaluating the term 'disorders of sex development' by implying in the question wording that the term is less appropriate for use with non-clinicians. In response to my question, the doctor indirectly aligned with this move by animating a stance bid on Chinese parents (also animated by Dr Law – Extract 3) evaluating them as likely to be pathologizers of their child's intersex variations. Investment in this negative evaluation of Chinese families is mitigated somewhat by the assertion (line 5) that they are '*not as traditional as before*', nevertheless, this stancetaking sequence does continue. Fung speaks of negatively evaluating the term abnormal to downplay its force ('*a variant to the usual kind of presentation but not exactly very abnormal*' – lines 9–10) to counter this pathologizing tendency and get parents to 'engage *in the management of the kid*' (lines 7–8). As follows, Fung builds into this stancetaking process the idea that clinicians should be shaping parent perceptions so that parents can be 'good' managers of their children.

Interviewer 2 then takes over for the Cantonese portion of the interview and revisits the topic of speaking to children (redacted for irrelevance to the analysis at hand). The topic soon returns to parents, with Interviewer 2 (lines 27–28) contributing to the earlier stancetaking process on parents by introducing social class, using implicature in the question to evaluate education level as producing a 'significant difference' in approach. Fung joins the sequence, aligning and showing high investment, saying it's 'very different' (line 30). Fung then goes on to assert that more highly educated parents can more readily absorb relevant concepts ('*the explanation feels much easier*' line 31). The reason given (lines 32–33) animates stancetaking in which a biological sex essence might express on the body's surface in 'deceiving' ways. That is, more highly educated parents can 'grasp' the idea that a person's sexual organs 'may or may not be like boys or girls' despite their 'essential' biological sex ('genetic male or female'). Intertwined with this stancetaking on intersex variations is another stancetaking process more relevant to the current section, stancetaking on parents. I will now focus more directly on that aspect.

Fung moves on from positive evaluation of parents from higher on the socioeconomic class scale (via their education) and begins instead to engage in stancetaking around parents perceived to be on the lower end of that scale (i.e., line 35 '*families of lower socioeconomic class*'). In lines 35–36, Fung initiates a negative evaluation, saying '*[T]hey might just become fixated on asking "So is this a boy or a girl", instead of understanding what is happening in the back*'. Although Fung goes on to further reinforce the negative evaluation by commenting on these parents' lesser ability to grasp unfamiliar terminology, for the purposes of analysis here, I would like to remain focused on the role of gender in this account. Fung engages in stancetaking on gender and on parents in a complex set of inflexions with lower socioeconomic class (and by implication lesser education). Such parents can make little sense of explanations in which gender (i.e., '*So is this a boy or a girl*' – line 36) and genetics ('understanding what is happening in the back' – lines 36–37) can mismatch. In other words, a stance seen in earlier analyses (Section 5) has little purchase with lower socioeconomic class parents. I refer to the stance in which genetics is positively evaluated as the source of everything, so a child can have, say, a genetic male biological sex essence but a girl's outward presentation (i.e., be a girl on the outside but a boy on the inside – see also Extract 9) (*cf* King, *forthcoming*). Fung highly invests in this negative stancetaking on parents, using the word 'fixate'(lines 35 and 41), implying their undue and irrational preoccupation with receiving a unitary either/or assessment. It prevents them from hearing other possibilities; they just want to skip the explanation and hear the final answer, which they assume will be an inevitable and tidy assessment of which side of the girl/boy binary the child is on despite any technical hitches. It is reminiscent of findings by Timmermans et al. (2019) in which clinicians and parents assume the child has a 'gender destiny' originating in their body's biology that just needs to be cultivated into line. Here, the assumption is projected mainly onto the parents, with lower socioeconomic class parents therefore '*at a different level actually*' (line 37) and so having much influence on them as perceiving subjects (i.e., shaping their perceptions of bodies and social roles) is challenging in this account. They are less malleable for being crafted into good parents (i.e., biopolitical managers) of their child with intersex variations. Of course, it would be another matter to discern whether being less reachable through scientific explanations necessarily prevents parents/families from perceiving their child's life as liveable without infant surgeries.

6.2 Discussion – Dr Fung

In lines 7–10, Dr Fung refers directly to getting parents to '*engage in the management of the kid*' and to maximize the chances of that happening, certain terms are avoided (e.g., *abnormal* or *disorder*). Fung is crafting subjects through a very nuanced spread of biomedical knowledge that floats at the border of English and Cantonese. Using biomedical terms in English, Fung suggests, is not as alarming to parents as the same terms translated into Cantonese, which clearly provides a very different kind of access way to understanding. It is akin to a phenomenon I have written about elsewhere (King, 2023b) in which opaque jargon terms can serve chiefly as reference (i.e., like names) rather than denoting or connoting biomedical information.

That is, they function in a more 'proprial' way (proper-noun-like). But for those who do understand what the jargon means, certain components (e.g., 'syndrome' or 'plasia') remain connected to the mental lexicon and carry associative and emotive meanings in ways that names (purely referential) do not (Nyström, 2016). It is interesting here to see that Fung talks about a similar divide between languages in Hong Kong (rather than between laypeople and experts), with Cantonese clearly providing denotations and connotations to the primarily Cantonese-speaking parent listeners that English does not, and this type of meaning-making is more difficult for clinicians to manage (similar to challenges reported by interpreters in hospitals – Lara-Otero et al., 2019). However, it is the doctor's account of attempts at management of linguistic and cultural hurdles that is most relevant here. Not necessarily inhibiting health communication, differences in spoken language and cultural beliefs can instead be negotiated in interaction, participants drawing on various communication strategies to resolve possible differences and misunderstandings with varying success (Zayts-Spence, Fung, and Chung, 2021). What I am consequently very occupied with during analysis are any stances and guiding ideologies that might be latent in their reported communication strategies but are detectable in the discourse of the interviews.

In sum, Fung starts off a stancetaking series by evaluating Chinese parents negatively and portraying them as pathologizers of intersex variations in their children, although admitting that they are less so than in the past. This parental perception must be altered somewhat. Intersex variations are then framed as deviating from their biological essence. More highly educated parents are much easier to influence because they can grasp this. Lesser-educated parents are less rational and cannot easily grasp that gender and genetics can mismatch. Thus, Fung's stance is that parents must not have their pathologizing perceptions ratified if they are to be good biopolitical managers. There is a sense, however, that their children can be boys or girls regardless of what their genetic makeup is, and so binary gender-sex is playing less of a regulatory role in the shaping of parents than it is in the shaping of intersex variations themselves.

6.3 Dr Ngai

The stancetaking in Ngai's account maintains a disease-based negative evaluation that contributes to pathologizing intersex variations, even while seeming to lessen the sense of urgency. The discussion repeats a 'psychosocial emergency' narrative, where medical intervention is presented as necessary relief for anxious parents. By deliberately using the English word *sex* instead of the English word *gender* or the Cantonese term for *sex*, Ngai emphasizes biological categorization and evades the idea of gender as a social construction. The omission of 'gender' and 'gender of rearing' points to an underlying assumption that surgical decisions based on fetal evidence resolve the problem. The persistent concern with identifying a child as either a boy or a girl shows how sex difference is mobilized to sustain the gender binary.

Prior to Extract 7, in the Cantonese portion of the interview, Dr Ngai had been responding to an interview question about the use of Cantonese versus English when speaking to parents. Dr Ngai had emphasized that Cantonese is always used when it is the parents' first language. Ngai had also asserted that with first-language English speakers they might use English terms from biomedicine such as 'differences of sex development' or 'disorders of sex development', but when speaking Cantonese would say something descriptive such as 'their development is different from other kids' instead of attempting a direct translation. Then, Interviewer 2 turns to asking about parent reactions.

Extract 7 (Dr Ngai)
(1) **INTERVIEWER 2**: *So you get similar reactions usually?*
(2) **NGAI**: *It's generally okay. But foreigners accept these DSD conditions a bit*
(3) *better usually, we feel*
(4) **INTERVIEWER 2**: *They take it easier*
(5) **NGAI**: *Yes. Yes. Exactly*
(6) **INTERVIEWER 2**: *So for Chinese parents, what strategies do you have to*
(7) *take things step by step*
(8) **NGAI**: *Mhm. Usually we won't talk about things in the future too far ahead*
(9) *first. Perhaps just what the treatment is for the moment. Usually we need to*
(10) *find the cause of DSD first, so the focus is usually on what investigation to*
(11) *be done to find out the cause of DSD. In the long run, like fertility issue or*
(12) *hormonal therapy, we won't talk about those right at the beginning right at*
(13) *birth. Otherwise, the family may feel a very heavy burden.*
(14) **INTERVIEWER 2**: *So this is the biggest difference? For English speakers*
(15) **NGAI**: *Actually it's more or less the same for English speakers*
(16) **INTERVIEWER 2**: *Same*
(17) **NGAI**: *Yes. Right. Unless the family comes to ask specifically, otherwise we*
(18) *won't talk about too much in the far future ahead. Maybe we will just wait*
(19) *until there's a very definitive diagnosis, then we'll talk about future problems*
(20) **INTERVIEWER 2**: *So, according to your experience and parents' reactions.*
(21) *Changes in your strategy, from the start, from the beginning . . .*
(22) **NGAI**: *As in . . .*
(23) **INTERVIEWER 2**: *Your experience in this aspect, have you learned a certain*
(24) *strategy?*

52   Language, Gender and Sexuality

(25) **NGAI**: *I think it is that we should not tell them too many things at a time.*
(26) *Maybe at first, when we started meeting the family, we tell them what's the*
(27) *disease, what's the problem, and everything about the disease. But I found*
(28) *out that parents are never able to take in that much information. Also, for*
(29) *things like getting married or giving birth, these are not things to consider*
(30) *this early to begin with, so there is no point to tell them these at that*
(31) *moment.*

In line 1, the interviewer responds to Ngai's prior stance bid in which they evaluated translation to Cantonese as best avoided in this context, asserting that parents need to be approached a bit differently depending on whether it is done in Cantonese or English. The interviewer joins the stancetaking process, querying parent reactions in a tone that evaluates reactions from Chinese parents as probably similar to the rest. Ngai aligns to this bid, but with low investment in line 2, saying only that '*It's generally okay*' and then changes course and disaligns from the evaluation, suggesting 'foreigners' accept it more easily but again with low investment – '*a bit*' – and distributing this stance among a generalized '*we*' who feel this way. Interviewer 2 then aligns to this stancetaking on Chinese parents and implies via the next question (line 6) that Chinese parents must require a more 'strategic' and gradual approach.

In lines 8–13, Ngai aligns with that evaluation ('*mhm*') and goes on to suggest that jumping ahead to the child's future prematurely (i.e., '*right at birth*') can impose a '*heavy burden*' on the family (investing more and enhancing the grave tone). Also, we see again the focus on finding the cause of the intersex variation so that a 'sex of rearing' can be assigned to the child. The apparatus of compulsory ablebodiedness and its entanglement with binary gender is still in evidence, as it was with Extract 5, but here I am more interested in the current focus – that is, what the account teaches us about the influencing of parent perceptions in the biopolitics of patient-centred medicine.

Ngai has built a stance in which parents of a child with intersex variations shoulder a heavy burden, attributing this burden to the mistake of raising topics like infertility or hormonal therapy too hastily. But there seems to be no related sense that clinicians talking about the child's body in a problem status, as 'diseased' or 'ill' also lays a heavy burden on them '*right at birth*'. Ngai then says that '*the parents are never able to take in that much information*' (line 28), but perhaps the reason clinicians lose parents is because their child is framed as a problem at the outset. Yet no mention of this possibility appears in the account. Extract 8 continues directly on from Extract 7, and the interviewer animates a stance bid in which the initial clinician reticence identified in lines 28–31 is evaluated to (possibly) be a consequence of the particular role their department colleagues play in the larger scheme.

> Extract 8 – (Dr Ngai cont'd)
> (32) **INTERVIEWER 2**: *So do you think it's because you're in [department*
> (33) *redacted], so you're not involved in this . . .*
> (34) **NGAI**: *Erm. Not really. It's just that the parents also need to accept a lot of*
> (35) *things right from the start. The child will be different from other normal kids,*
> (36) *the parents will have a lot to worry about. They may be some new parents*
> (37) *themselves, and there are a lot for them to accept just for that. So, it's*
> (38) *actually most important to emphasize that the child is not in life-threatening*
> (39) *condition at the moment, that he is stable. Things that are not urgent can be*
> (40) *left for later. Unless it's something that affects how we determine the sex.*
> (41) *Like in some condition, the boy will become infertile, then if the parents*
> (42) *think really being infertile means they don't want to rear that person as a*
> (43) *boy, and should be reared as a girl, then these will be discussed earlier on.*
> (44) *Otherwise, when there's not even a very definitive diagnosis, we won't talk*
> (45) *so much about future issues.*
> (46) **INTERVIEWER 2**: *So the last question is about this term "intersex". Would*
> (47) *any parent go online to search about it?*
> (48) **NGAI**: *They do, I guess. We don't use that term anymore, however. Yeh, we*
> (49) *don't. But when the parents view online, they might still see a lot of*
> (50) *information with this term. Maybe for older information. They will still ask.*
> (51) *Then, we also explain: Actually, now, we commonly have a more precise*
> (52) *'sex of rearing', and not intersex. Even if he is reared as a boy, it is different.*
> (53) *[That is], if it is decided he is to be reared as male, then he is a male with*
> (54) *some differences in genitalia rather than intersex. Not to be considered*
> (55) *"neither-boy-or-girl". He is just a boy with some differences.*

In line 34, Ngai disaligns from this evaluation ('Erm, not really') and goes on to keep building the stance that pointed to Chinese parents bearing a particularly heavy parental burden, saying that they need to 'accept a lot of things right from the start' and first of all just need to know that the child is safe. It seems reasonable to address the fact that parents, in some cases *new* parents moreover, will need to process the child's innate difference from most kids. Furthermore, Ngai is building into the stancetaking a positive evaluation of the idea that acceptance of this parenting reality should be the top priority before getting into decisions about sex of rearing and fertility. In other words, Ngai creates a stance where, until the child has been accepted, it is best not to bombard parents with such big challenges.

6.4 Discussion – Dr Ngai

Up to this point, the disease framing has been taken completely for granted by Ngai, but it is problematic to suggest that one is softening the pathologization by removing a sense of urgency. Along the way, there is a catastrophizing discourse built into this account that evokes the 'psychosocial emergency' stance that has been so commonly identified as problematic (seen in Section 5). In lines 39–40, Ngai further defines topics to be deferred by excluding sex assignment from the list *'Things that are not urgent can be left for later. Unless it's something that affects how we determine the sex'*. There is a Cantonese word that translates as 'sex' but no Cantonese word for gender, so in the Hong Kong context, the English term 'gender' is used (either a transference or borrowing). What is most interesting is that Ngai actually opts to insert the English word 'sex' here (除非佢會係影響我地 *determine* 個 *sex* 個啲), instead of the Cantonese word for sex, which they also do with the phrase 'sex of rearing' in line 52 (講都會有個好確切嘅 *sex of rearing*). This means there can be no sense of ambiguous translation – Ngai has avoided using *gender* and *gender of rearing*, an omission that hints strongly that they are talking about surgically altering the children's bodies according to the foetal development evidence, not just deciding the gender to assign until the child is old enough to decide. Through this focus on sex, we see in the stancetaking process that coming forth with a diagnosis on either side of the sex difference binary, and most probably irreversible assignment surgery, is still the way to alleviate this parental burden, or this psychosocial emergency. The overriding question 'Is it a boy or a girl?' is still driving this whole enterprise, so gender is ultimately the apparatus of bioregulation that sits behind it all. The apparatus of sex difference is put to the service of the gender binary, as a way to reassure parents that the chosen gender of rearing has a basis in science.

6.5 Dr Au

In the coming excerpts from the interview with Dr Au, the main insight is the tracking of stancetaking by which the affective experience of parents is managed through a process of interpreting their *reactions* as certain *emotions* (i.e., you're feeling *this*, it means *that*). Although ostensibly necessary for keeping parents engaging and not despairing, this guided interpretation of how to rationalise how they feel is indicative of biopolitics influencing subjecthood. Also, while negatively evaluating XX/XY determinism and positively evaluating gender as an emancipatory force that can free individuals from genetic essentialism, their stancetaking still reproduces pathologizing logics that label intersex bodies as 'abnormal'. Medical culture's professional ethos, which is rooted in biopower, demands intervention and correction, reinforcing compulsory able-bodiedness and binary gender norms. Ultimately, Dr Au demonstrates how even well-intentioned clinicians and parents become enmeshed in regulatory discourses that construct and sustain abnormality discourse despite a professed desire to alleviate stigma.

Prior to Extract 9, in response to the interviewer's prompting, Dr Au had been talking about various approaches to explaining innate sex characteristics, including drawings and diagrams along with verbal descriptions. While gauging the response of the parents, Dr Au claimed to explain genetic concepts and anatomical processes to help them understand what was considered by clinicians to be the norm in sexual differentiation and what was not, and where their child's body fit. The interviewer then prompted Dr Au to demonstrate such an explanation, leading to a series of extended turns at talk, with the interviewer mainly backchanneling to signal attentiveness.

Extract 9 (Dr Au)
(1) **INTERVIEWER 2**: *If I were a patient or the patient's parents, how*
(2) *would you explain my condition to me, where would you start?*
(3) *AU: I think I need to use two examples because they are quite different.*
(4) **INTERVIEWER 2**: *mhm, right*
(lines 5–30 redacted for lack of relevance to Section 6)
(31) *AU: Another difficult situation for parents would be knowing that the patient*
(32) *is, in fact, 46XY.*
(33) **INTERVIEWER 2**: *mhm*
(34) *AU: When they visit, it's usually a very tall girl*
(35) **INTERVIEWER 2**: *Yes*
(36) *AU: and we'll see, oh, she doesn't have much body hair and that's already*
(37) *peculiar. Then, after a karyotype test, we find out they have XY*
(38) **INTERVIEWER 2**: *ohh*
(39) *AU: so, in fact, they should be a boy, but they may have androgen*
(40) *insensitivity since birth*
(41) **INTERVIEWER 2**: *mhm*
(42) *AU: which renders them insensitive to male hormones. So, he had always*
(43) *appeared to be a girl until now; these are usually complete AIS.*
(44) **INTERVIEWER 2**: *mhm mhm*
(45) *AU: This kind of case is difficult. I need to explain it much more skilfully*
(46) *because the mum and dad – you tell them it's XY, with some knowledge,*
(47) *they will already say, "What? Oh, so it's a boy." They'll be in shock*
(48) **INTERVIEWER 2**: *mhm*

(49) *AU: Whatever you tell them after that point will be filtered and not heard.*
(50) **INTERVIEWER 2**: *ohhh*
(51) *AU: This is how I see parents react usually. Yes, it's hard.*

To start with, in line 3, Dr Au decides to divide the explanation into two parts, and this partition is according to whether the 'biological sex' of the child is deemed to be female or male (regardless of outward appearance), based on a key pair of chromosomes that is either XX (female) or XY (male). The redacted part of Au's explanation is about a condition called MRKH,[5] which causes the vagina and uterus to be underdeveloped or absent in someone who has XX as the key chromosome pair. They have functioning ovaries and otherwise outwardly appear female except for the absence of menstrual periods due to the lack of a uterus or its lack of function. Au animates a stance bid with the assertion that these cases are straightforward to explain to parents (relative to the case analysed below) because the key chromosome pair (i.e., XX) and the child's outward appearance (i.e., girl) match sociocultural expectations. Their child's status as a girl remains stable, and it does not occur to parents to question it. In Au's account, the process in this case becomes mainly a matter of addressing questions around assisted reproductive technology as well as concerns about vaginal shape and function. This last point is an important one, for surgery on children's vaginas has been extremely controversial because it is a major surgery with potential for serious complications, and there have been continual calls for it to be deferred so that the individuals can weigh risks vs benefits for themselves (Earp and Steinfeld, 2018). Au only briefly alludes to this topic, though, and it is not relevant to this section's focus on parent subjecthood.

In lines 31–32, Au bolsters the stancetaking process around the second part of the explanation, which addresses XY cases rather than XX. They animate a stance bid in which identification of a daughter's key chromosome pair as XY is evaluated negatively, as a '*difficult situation for parents*'. In lines 34–40, Au describes how sometimes a rather tall teenage girl arrives in the examination room because her puberty appears to be delayed ('*she doesn't have much body hair and that's already peculiar*' – lines 36–37). Then it is discovered (via a Karyotype test) that her key chromosome pair is XY, and Au states in line 39, '*so, in fact, they should be a boy*'. By saying '*should*' Au animates a stance that has emerged previously in this study, by evaluating the Y chromosome as representing a biological essence (see also Richardson, 2013). That is, the presence of XY means that the patient is a girl

---

[5] Mayer-Rokitansky-Küster-Hauser syndrome.

on the outside but a boy on the inside, housed out of sight, deep in the chromosomes.

Au goes on to say that the patient has probably had androgen insensitivity since birth, meaning that the body's hormone receptors responded to steroid hormones (e.g., testosterone, dihydrotestosterone and androstenedione) in a limited way, so they were not detected by the body at a high enough level to cause the formation of a penis, scrotum and prostate in utero, or to produce masculine secondary sex characteristics in puberty (i.e., deepened voice timbre, v-shaped torso, etc). Au in line 42 explains it a bit differently, negatively evaluating their bodies, saying that this '*renders them insensitive to male hormones*', which is another example of a zombie fact (see Section 5) being used to talk about bodies. They are not 'male hormones' because they are also substantial in the female body; it is the amount that tips the scales, not the presence. Dr Au undoubtedly knows this fact but in this account chooses to repeat the outdated and problematic 'male hormone' discourse.

The stancetaking process is picked up again in lines 42–43, as Au evaluates the outward body as being deceptive, '*he had always appeared to be a girl until now*,' further developing the stance bid by using the pronoun '*he*' and stating that the child has merely '*appeared*' to be a girl but is not one. This begs the question of what makes a girl a girl. It is a question that, to be fair, Au begins to unpack with more nuance in the rest of the account.

Au begins another stancetaking sequence in which simply to '*tell them it's XY*' (line 46) is evaluated negatively as an unskilful explanation because '*with some knowledge, they will already say, "What? Oh, so it's a boy". They'll be in shock*'. In other words, the implicature here is that 'XY' as a term calls forth the concept 'boy' for parents. It is because they have '*some knowledge*', and Au does not specify whether that means knowledge from their past schooling or knowledge just provided by the doctor. To bolster this evaluation, Au suggests that '*Whatever you tell them after that point will be filtered and not heard*' (line 49), increasing investment in the stancetaking through affect. Interviewer 2 aligns to this tone by replying '*ohhh*', a discourse marker that shows engagement in the conversation but also signals that some new information is unanticipated (Schiffrin, 1987), and its elongation adds emphasis. Au picks up the implicature from the interjection and replies, '*Yes, it's hard*' (line 51), setting a yet more sober tone. The effect of this short stancetaking exchange is to further develop the evaluation that explaining these cases to parents requires extra care, attention and skill. The reason that it requires extra skill is because of a need to manage the parents' affective experience (i.e., '*shock*') and keep the explanation within a boundary that keeps them listening and not despairing, guiding them towards ratified perceptions of what they are feeling. Au continues in Extract 10, which is an immediate continuation, and a clash of stances emerges in the account. The doctor continues to animate stance bids that say XY means a male essence but then disaligns from this evaluation repeatedly in a paradoxical fashion.

Extract 10 (Dr Au cont'd)
(52) *AU: So, I might start like this. Well, if we have some basic concept of how we*
(53) *distinguish boys and girls, then we can ask them if they knew there are 23*
(54) *pairs of chromosomes*
(55) **INTERVIEWER 2**: *mhm*
(56) *AU: half from dad and half from mum, 46 in total, 23 pairs. The last pair is*
(57) *how we determine the sex: XX for girls and XY for boys. So I need to make*
(58) *sure they understand this.*
(59) **INTERVIEWER 2**: *Yes*
(60) *AU: And from the report, we found out that your little girl is 46XY – they*
(61) *should be in shock at this point, like "so, you mean she's a boy?" This is*
(62) *where you need to explain*
(63) **INTERVIEWER 2**: *mhm*
(64) *AU: In fact, for all of our bodily appearance and reactions, her being XY*
(65) *means she should have developed into a boy, but when she lacks a few*
(66) *reactions, like an electrical switch that is not flipped*
(67) **INTERVIEWER 2**:*mhm*
(68) *AU: then they won't go the direction of a boy. The body has no reaction*
(69) *towards male hormones, so they went to the side of female development.*
(70) *So, if she was raised as a girl*
(71) **INTERVIEWER 2**: *mhm*
(72) *AU: then she still is a girl, but the body's cells and genes are XY, then some*
(73) *of the organs may be different from that of girls, maybe not developed*
(74) **INTERVIEWER 2**: *mhm*
(75) *AU: like the uterus. Legally, she is a girl, she still is a girl, like anyone else,*
(76) *we can be sure that she is a girl. But given the medical condition, I need to*
(77) *discuss with you things like her reproduction, or menstruation, or, for her*
(78) *organs – for us girls, that would be an ovary, but for XY-girls, she would have*
(79) *a testis. If it's not needed, we need to operate on it for removal because it*
(80) *may turn out to be harmful. After that, since there is a lack of organs for*
(81) *secreting growth hormones, she will need to take some hormone*
(82) *supplements.*
(83) **INTERVIEWER 2**: *mhm*
(84) *AU: As for why she has not shown any problems until now, that would be*
(85) *because the body failed to recognize the male hormone, which converts to*
(86) *female hormones. This is why her other developments are same as other*
(87) *girls, and she may be a bit taller. So, after the operation, we need to provide*
(88) *some hormone supplements. As for, in the future, things like marriage,*
(89) *relationships, giving birth, we really need to handle step by step; I think her*

(90) *thoughts have not reached that far yet. And we won't have only one*
(91) *consultation*
(92) **INTERVIEWER 2**: *oh, right*
(93) *AU: later on, so we can discuss each time*
(94) **INTERVIEWER 2**: *mhm*
(95) *AU: and see how much of it they have taken in . . . because it's already a lot*
(96) *for them to take in.*
(97) **INTERVIEWER 2**: *Yeah*

In lines 52–58, Au again animates the stance bid that an XY pair of chromosomes represents a biological essence and a male biological sex (*'XX for girls and XY for boys'* – line 57) and shows investment by stating that it is very important for the doctor to *'make sure they understand this'*, creating a tone of gravity. On the other hand, Au then goes on in the account to mitigate this stancetaking, disaligning from it somewhat. In line 60, Au implies that parents will then jump to a conclusion (*'so, you mean she's a boy?'*), and the doctor must intervene to dissuade them from this perception (even though Au has just said that XY means a boy). Although again animating the stance bid evaluating their daughter's body as unruly (i.e., not doing what it *'should'* do – line 59), Au uses a metaphor of non-flipped switches to explain that female development undeniably occurred despite the XY pair of chromosomes. What is implied here is that the flipping (or not) of the body's switches is also biologically foundational. This means *'she still is a girl'* (line 72), and an intertwined evaluation is forming in which XX and XY genes are not the sole determiners of boyhood vs. girlhood or even male vs. female. This stancetaking is compatible with contemporary science, as explained in Sections 2 and 5. Au continues building the stance that the daughter is nevertheless a girl, saying *'Legally, she is a girl, she still is a girl, like anyone else, we can be sure that she is a girl'* (lines 75–76). Au's point to the hypothetical parents is that this means she is indeed a girl, but because of the chromosomal XY makeup, some parts of her body are different from the majority of girls. Au is suggesting that if someone looks like a girl and is raised like a girl, and presumably *feels* like a girl, she is indeed a girl. However, this evaluation sits in great tension with the intertwined stancetaking process that keeps evaluating the child's body as unruly and wanting repair because it has been disobedient of its genetic XX/XY makeup. It is a highly problematic discourse that, according to Au, serves mainly to muddy the waters when talking to parents, and it must be asked whether it is instructive or even accurate. Or perhaps it is mainly evidence of biopolitical management of parent perceptions to soften them up for making 'choices' about childhood surgeries, a topic that Au goes on to mention.

Au could have left the account at that, with genetic sex determinism kept at bay and parents left reassured that their daughter is indeed a daughter despite some internal anatomical differences. Instead, they turn to animating a stance bid evaluating prophylactic gonadectomy (i.e., removal of internal testes) as advisable. Addressing the testis, Au says in lines 79–80, '*If it's not needed, we need to operate on it for removal because it may turn out to be harmful*', positioning themselves as principal via '*we*' and striking a neutral, matter-of-fact tone that frames the evaluation as fact, these moves combining to indicate alignment and investment in the stance being built. This '*need to operate*' is a zombie fact rather than a scientifically established fact, with a dearth of evidence to support it (Tack et al., 2019; Guerrero-Fernández et al., 2022; Ussher et al., 2024; Ho et al., 2025). Au goes on to suggest that after removal '*since there is a lack of organs for secreting growth hormones, she will need to take some hormone supplements*' (lines 80–82). No explanation is offered to reconcile how a testis is judged to be '*not needed*' when its removal subsequently necessitates hormone replacement therapy. Could her body not just be left alone?

6.6 Discussion – Dr Au

In the words of Liao (2022, p. 248), 'The biogenetic framing of DSD means that narratives of intersex are intrinsically pathology-centred and the care process technology-bound'. Biogenetic framing refers to XX/XY deterministic notions of male vs. female and pious beliefs by which 'Adam and Eve' reside stalwartly in our genes despite the 'deceptions' of observable body traits. Evidence in the current study furthermore shows that clinicians cannot resist pathologizing intersex variations even when, like Dr Au, they build stances against biogenetic framings. Au's account outlines attempts to shape parent perceptions, moulding them into good biopolitical managers of their children, but it is a paradoxical crafting, a mixture of keeping parents on-side but also driven by the imperative to 'find' abnormality and 'fix' it (DeLaet, Earp, and Mills, 2024). Compulsory ablebodiedness is certainly at play here, a biopolitical apparatus that keeps arising in clinicians' accounts and binding them to pathologization of intersex variations. But does gender also play a role? Is it emancipatory or regulatory or both? In the account given, Dr Au does, without a doubt, say that a child whose body formed as female and is raised as a girl is *still a girl* regardless of any new revelations about her internal physiology, biochemistry, or genetic makeup. Gender is setting the girl free of biogenetic determinism in this account, emancipating her. But then again, binary gender and biological sex, as regulatory biopolitical apparatuses, keep a fast hold on one another via the presence of XY in the account. She may be a girl, may even be female, but she is *abnormal* nonetheless because of her body's structural features, even though '*she has not shown any problems until now*' (line 84). Abnormality cannot easily be left alone in the corridors of medicine because medical training instils as professional values (a) the imperative to intervene on the body, and (b) a conviction that all 'abnormalities' can and must be corrected (Mishler, 1984). In other words, biopower has shaped these values, and they have also influenced layperson perceptions (see Section 3.2). Moreover, abnormalities are created by the discourse in those same corridors, sometimes unwittingly or even despite best efforts to avoid it.

7 Conclusion

My investigation has been guided by asking about the ways in which clinicians engage with innate sex characteristics, patients and families in their accounts of practice, and to determine whether their stancetaking is shaped by relations of biopower connecting gender, sexual difference, racialization and ableism. I also set out to trace moments in their stancetaking where intersex variations and subjects appear to break free from such biopolitical forces, exposing the emancipatory potential of gendering and interpret what these stances reveal to me about the institutional and personal ideologies that shape the viability and livability of intersex bodies and identities. In amongst these considerations has been my ongoing exploration of the continuing usefulness of *gender* in tandem with *biopolitics*.

In asking these questions, my aim has been to advance knowledge of how networks of structuring forces in the medical domain are in tension with the formation of intersex variations as well as parents and patients as subjects, shaping intersex experience. Analysis of these interviews has revealed that the fused regulatory apparatuses of gender, ableism and biological sex difference are indispensable for making sense of the bioregulation of innate sex characteristics and the consequences for the livable lives of people with intersex variations. I asked how those structures entered these accounts via discourse in interview stancetaking as an affective practice (Kiesling, 2018), and what this might imply for children with intersex variations, their parents and for clinicians. I examined stancetaking processes on innate sex characteristics as well as on parents and their families, asking whether biopower was evident. This procedure involved analysing stancetaking in the interview accounts, looking for signals of any regulatory influence of gender, dis/ability, ethnicity, gender, race, sex and socioeconomic class. I also asked how intersex variations and affected subjects might be unbound from biopolitics in these stances. I framed this as looking for openings to *esperançar*, or reflexive and pragmatic hopeful action.

As stated in the opening of Section 3, a stancetaking analysis conducted along the lines of interactional sociolinguistics permits a microanalysis of accounts to uncover a complex web of norms and resistance. The triadic stancetaking model proved highly useful because it treats stancetaking as an *activity* that unfolds across multiple turns in talk and sometimes in interaction between speakers in the interview. By making use of Goffman's notion of footing (i.e., authors, animators and principals), I saw a clearer picture come into view of how institutional stances play a significant role, but furthermore, nuances of how those stances are brought into the interaction revealed latent information that would have been missed in a less exacting version of qualitative analysis. Institutional stances can be brought up (animated) but more or less aligned to, and more or less responsibility can be taken for animating those stances. Furthermore, nuances can be woven in by adjusting the degree of alignment with the animated stance's evaluation(s) and the affective tone that is struck (i.e., level of investment in the animated stance).

In this grid of options, important subtleties of communication become clear that can give crucial clues about the ideologies behind a speaker's words that might not match the outward message. An example is the stance process in Extract 4, where Dr Law animated an institutional stance from biomedicine, positively evaluating the idea that predicting gender identity from a specific diagnosis of intersex variation can be done reliably. By striking a mitigating tone, Law does not fully align, developing a more nuanced evaluation in which anatomy is not *necessarily* destiny and predicting gender identity is actually an imprecise practice, placing some importance on the patient's own *feeling* (lived experience). Closer scrutiny revealed, however, that Law ultimately does align with a positive evaluation of the biologically deterministic notion that the patient's body shapes those feelings. This is akin to findings in Timmermans et al. (2019, p. 1531) where, in clinician discourse, a gender lurks in the child but requires cultivation with biomedical nurturing and parental socialization (a discourse that the researchers call 'Gender Destinies'). Without uncovering the nuances of the interviewee as animator performing alignments and investments, the full raft of insights around discourses of 'gender destiny' would not have come to light in this case. So, I argue that Interactional sociolinguistic discourse analysis holds great promise for future contributions to critical intersex studies.

Regardless of their intentions, clinicians are ultimately potential agents of biopolitical management, and the effect of their gendered ableist discourse in hospitals is to steer parents of children with intersex variations in ways clinicians might not even realize. Their medical expertise leads them to align to stances whose affect and evaluation end up latent in talk rather than overt, stances often not noticeable to analysts deploying higher-level coding techniques. Furthermore, these clinician alignments can emerge from certitude but at other times from a need to signal membership in a clinician discourse community via acquiescence. In other words, they end up 'talking the talk' (and presumably 'walking the walk') of the institution to maintain credibility amongst their peers. Patient-centred shared decision-making is a process meant, in its most ideal enactments, to give parents freedom of choice, but they might instead be left feeling bereft of options and fully responsible for any consequences (Crocetti, Berry, and Monro, 2024). Stripped of authority in one sense, clinicians end up coaching parents anyway via interaction, weaving institutional stance bids into their explanations via the back door (Davis and Murphy, 2013), imbuing stance bids with evaluations and emotional tones that serve as directive cues to parents. These challenges with patient-centred medicine exist across medical practice (Pilnick, 2022), but their relevance looms large in relation to the pathologization of innate sex characteristics. In the words of prominent bio-ethicist Anita Ho, 'In an ableist society, we need to ask whether or how many personal decisions are shaped by the dominant culture. To truly promote autonomy, we need to restructure the social framework to ensure that people's preferences are not foreclosed because of discriminatory attitudes and oppressive social structure' (Ho, 2008, p. 205). This verdict applies to intersex variations.

There is a stance that repeatedly emerges in the accounts via positive evaluation of the outdated notion that a Y chromosome represents a biological essence. That is, the presence of XY means that the patient can 'appear' to be a girl on the outside but is actually a boy on the inside, housed out of sight, deep in the chromosomes (yet another biopolitical manifestation of 'gender destiny' as a self-fulfilling prophecy – Timmermans et al., 2019). Outward bodies are framed as deceiving things. There are moments when gender seems to shine a light of *hope* in the accounts, surgery framed as unnecessary because the gender of rearing can provide control to parents instead. But even in these accounts, although it is acknowledged that gender can be *felt* by someone, biological sex is ultimately said to set the agenda for those feelings via binary genetics. Gender's potential is curtailed, and hopeful action outside of surgery is erased. A girl with the XY genetic marker may be a girl, may even be female, but she is nonetheless said to be abnormal.

The birth of children with intersex variations is, in one clinician's account, negatively evaluated as an emergency and emoted as one of utmost urgency, a stance animated from within biomedicine. Yet this stance, imbued with affect, is also ascribed more than once in the data to Chinese parents, who are said to be particularly enthusiastic pathologizers who must be put in their place (along the way, constructing Hong Kong culture as the driver). But parents must not have their pathologizing perceptions ratified if they are to be good biopolitical managers. Furthermore, the crafting of parent subjects in Hong Kong is said to sit awkwardly at the border of English and Cantonese. Cantonese provides denotations and connotations to the primarily Cantonese-speaking parent listeners that English does not, and this type of meaning-making is more difficult for clinicians to manage. Furthermore, news of an intersex variation is said to be a heavy burden for parents because of their expectations about their child's future and that of the family. A stance emerged via high investment in a positive evaluation of clinicians actively managing the parents' affective experience (i.e., 'shock') and keeping the explanation within a boundary that keeps them listening and not despairing, guiding them towards ratified perceptions of what they are feeling. Then again, the clinicians' own tendency to stand in white coats and speak in terms of disease and illness right from the start is repeatedly the 'elephant in the room' in these interviews and might actually be the fundamental burden. This possibility does not enter into the accounts, however.

At the root of these stances lies ableism via the affective 'catastrophizing' of non-malignant bodily variations, but binary gender and biological sex are entangled together and fused with ableism. As suggested in the opening paragraphs of this Element, maintaining a manifold view of the processes of subject/body formation and 'biopolitics in action' is necessary as part of a re-emphasis of gender as relevant and transformative – both a system of power and a lived reality. I have argued that gender operates as both an enabling and constraining force within biomedical and biopolitical frameworks, shaping population management as a mechanism of governance, but remaining emancipatory in affirming diverse, resistant lived experiences. This dual role is crucial for fostering liveable lives for people with intersex variations, especially within healthcare communication, where gender both structures and challenges prevailing norms.

The analysis here demonstrates gender's usefulness. There are moments in the stancetaking evaluations and alignments of some of these clinicians when the livability of intersex variations is tied to gender as a lived reality, anchored to bodily integrity and autonomy, and not requiring surgery on minors. These moments are fleeting, however, and entangled with the animation of institutional discourses that maintain the centrality of a biological sex essence lodged in the Y chromosome despite a lack of support for this version of sex in up-to-date science. These accounts are important because they open a portal into the meeting place between subjectivities and bodies and overlapping biopolitical apparatuses in action, all of which *have* combined, *would* combine, or *will* combine to shape intersex experience. At this meeting place, it is possible to see in these accounts how parent subjectivity (i.e., the 'good' biopolitical parent manager) and intersex embodiment (i.e., intersex variations of innate sex characteristics) are shaped in gendering, sexing and dis/ableizing processes that are a product of strategies of governmentality (i.e., the roundabout shaping of human conduct). But they are also the site of potential resistance via gender, which by necessity starts with people's purposeful destabilizations of normalized subjectivities and embodiments.

Where does this leave us in terms of levelling the path to the livability of lives for all people with intersex variations? Intersex bio-ethicist Morgan Carpenter has argued that stakeholders can, if truth be told, agree to disagree about the foundations of sex as long as there is firm commitment to fundamental human rights norms and standards (2022). Such a commitment entails ' ... promoting specific attention to intersex-specific human rights abuses and specific community resourcing needs, and by documenting abuses, disentangling misconceptions, and promoting practical reforms that implement human rights protections in medical and social settings' (p. 179). It is my hope that the analysis in this study assists with disentangling misconceptions in the Hong Kong context and beyond.

That said, there is a great need for more interactional sociolinguistic research (indeed, any social science research) analysing actual clinician-parent and clinician-patient interactions inside the consultation room. There are crucial ethical questions to address in embarking on recording and transcribing such interactions, but clinician-patient interaction is a robust area of research with countless precedents to follow. To suggest that intersex variations make the prospect prohibitively daunting would be to bolster their framing as a deeply embarrassing psychosocial emergency, a discourse that I am loath to perpetuate. The genie is now out of the bottle, and as the public gains increasing awareness of intersex variations, there will be an increasing number of cases where parents and their children with intersex variations, and also adults with intersex variations, chart their own course of *esperançar*, their own muscular, hopeful action to build liveable lives outside of the gendered ableist assumptions of biomedicine. If called upon by people with intersex variations, or brave clinicians who care about and prioritize bodily integrity and autonomy, sociolinguists have tools to bring to the table in seeking to know how hopeful action unfolds in the corridors and institutions of biomedicine, or perhaps most importantly, beyond them.

References

Agamben, G. (1995) *Homo sacer: Sovereign power and bare life*. Translated by D. Heller-Roazen. Stanford, CA: Stanford University Press.

Agamben, G. (2005) *State of exception*. Translated by K. Attell. Chicago: University of Chicago Press.

Ainsworth, C. (2015) 'Sex redefined', *Nature*, 518(7539), pp. 288–291.

Baratz, A. B. and Feder, E. K. (2015) 'Misrepresentation of evidence favoring early normalizing surgery for atypical sex anomalies', *Archives of Sexual Behavior*, 44(7), pp. 1761–1763.

Barrett, R. and Hall, K. (2023) 'Closet monsters: Naysayers, gatekeepers, and bullies in queer and trans linguistics', in T. E. Kibbey (ed.) *Linguistics out of the closet: The interdisciplinarity of gender and sexuality in language science*. Berlin: De Gruyter Mouton, pp. 259–276.

Birke, L. (1999) *Feminism and the biological body*. Edinburgh: Edinburgh University Press.

Bonnin, J.E. (2013) 'New dimensions of linguistic inequality: An overview', *Language and Linguistics Compass*, 7(9), pp. 500–509.

Borba, R. (2019) 'The interactional making of a "true transsexual": Language and (dis)identification in trans-specific healthcare', *International Journal of the Sociology of Language*, 256, pp. 21–55.

Borba, R. (2022) 'Enregistering "gender ideology": The emergence and circulation of a transnational anti-gender language', *Journal of Language and Sexuality*, 11(1), pp. 57–79.

Borba, R., Hall, K. and Hiramoto, M. (2020) 'Editorial: Feminist refusal meets enmity', *Gender and Language*, 14(1), pp. 1–7.

Butler, J. (1993) *Bodies that matter: On the discursive limits of 'sex'*. London: Routledge.

Butler, J. (2004) *Undoing gender*. London: Routledge.

Butler, J. (2015) *Notes toward a performative theory of assembly*. Cambridge, MA: Harvard University Press.

Canagarajah, S. (2022) *Language incompetence: Learning to communicate through cancer, disability, and anomalous embodiment*. Abingdon: Routledge.

Canagarajah, S. (2023) 'A decolonial crip linguistics', *Applied Linguistics*, 44(1), pp. 1–21.

Carpenter, M. (2012) 'Intersex: Intersectionalities with disabled people', *Intersex Human Rights Australia*, 29 October.

Carpenter, M. (2016) 'The human rights of intersex people: Addressing harmful practices and rhetoric of change', *Reproductive Health Matters*, 24(47), pp. 74–84.

Carpenter, M. (2018) 'The "normalisation" of intersex bodies and "othering" of intersex identities', in J. M. Scherpe, A. Dutta and T. Helms (eds) *The legal status of intersex persons*. Cambridge: Intersentia, pp. 445–514.

Carpenter, M. (2022) 'Intersex human rights in a time of instrumentalization and backlash', in A. T. Chase, P. Mahdavi, H. Banai and S. Gruskin (eds) *Human rights at the intersections: Transformation through local, global, and cosmopolitan challenges*. London: Bloomsbury, pp. 169–179.

Carpenter, M. (2024) 'Fixing bodies and shaping narratives: Epistemic injustice and the responses of medicine and bioethics to intersex human rights demands', *Clinical Ethics*, 19(1), pp. 3–17.

Carpenter, M., Kraus, C. and Earp, B. D. (2024) 'Reply to Hadidi', *Journal of Pediatric Urology*, 20(3), pp. 435–436.

Case, M. A. (2019) 'Trans formations in the Vatican's war on "gender ideology"', *Signs*, 44(3), pp. 639–664.

Chan-Yeung, M. M. W. (2018) *A medical history of Hong Kong: 1842–1941*. Hong Kong: The Chinese University of Hong Kong Press.

Chase, C. (2003) 'What is the agenda of the intersex patient advocacy movement?' *The Endocrinologist*, 13(3), pp. 240–242.

Clare, E. (2017) *Brilliant imperfection: Grappling with cure*. Durham: Duke University Press.

Clune-Taylor, C. (2020) 'Is sex socially constructed?' in S. Crasnow and K. Intemann (eds) *The Routledge handbook of feminist philosophy of science*. Abingdon: Routledge, pp. 187–200.

Cornwall, S. (2013) 'Asking about what is better: Intersex, disability, and inaugurated eschatology', *Journal of Religion, Disability, and Health*, 17(4), pp. 369–392.

Crocetti, D. and Prandelli, M. (2024) 'Navigating parental decision-making: Intersex surgeries in italy', *Social Science & Medicine*, 363(117496), pp. 1–8.

Crocetti, D., Berry, A. and Monro, S. (2024) 'Navigating the complexities of adult healthcare for individuals with variations of sex characteristics: From paediatric emergencies to a sense of abandonment', *Culture, Health & Sexuality*, 26(3), pp. 332–345.

Crocetti, D., Garland, F., Griffiths, D.A. (2024) 'Editorial introduction to centring intersex issues: Global and local dimensions', *Social Sciences*, 13(11), p. 602.

Davis, G. (2015) *Contesting intersex: The dubious diagnosis.* New York: New York University Press.

Davis, G. and Murphy, E. L. (2013) 'Intersex bodies as states of exception: An empirical explanation for unnecessary genital modification', *Feminist Formations*, 25(2), pp. 129–152.

Davis, G. and Preves, S. (2020) 'Reflecting on intersex: 25 years of activism, mobilization, and change', in C. G. Valentine, M. N. Trautner and J. Z. Spade (eds) *The kaleidoscope of gender: Prisms, patterns, and possibilities.* 6th ed. Thousand Oaks, CA: Sage, pp. 25–36.

Davis, J. L., Zimman, L. and Raclaw, J. (2014) 'Opposites attract: Retheorizing binaries in language, gender, and sexuality', in L. Zimman, J. L. Davis and J. Raclaw (eds) *Queer excursions: Retheorizing binaries in language, gender, and sexuality.* New York: Oxford University Press, pp. 1–12.

DeLaet, D. L., Earp, B. D. and Mills, E. (2024) 'Which children have rights? The child's right to bodily integrity and protection gaps for children with intersex traits under international and national laws', *Amicus Curiae*, 5(3), pp. 448–473.

Delimata, N. (2019) *Articulating intersex: A crisis at the intersection of scientific facts and social ideals.* Cham: Springer.

Dice, L. R. (1952) 'Heredity clinics: Their value for public service and for research', *American Journal of Human Genetics*, 4(1), pp. 1–13.

Du Bois, J. W. (2007) 'The stance triangle', in R. Englebretson (ed.) *Stancetaking in discourse: Subjectivity, evaluation, interaction.* Amsterdam: John Benjamins, pp. 139–182.

Du Bois, J. W. and Kärkkäinen, E. (2012) 'Taking a stance on emotion: Affect, sequence, and intersubjectivity in dialogic interaction', *Text & Talk*, 32(4), pp. 433–451.

Earp, B. D. and Steinfeld, R. (2018) 'Genital autonomy and sexual well-being', *Current Sexual Health Reports*, 10, pp. 7–17.

Eckert, L. (2017) *Intersexualization: The clinic and the colony.* Abingdon: Routledge.

Ellison, T., Green, K.M., Richardson, M. and Snorton, C.R. (2017) 'We got issues: Toward a Black trans*/studies', *Transgender Studies Quarterly*, 4(2), pp. 162–169.

Englebretson, R. (2023) 'Epilogue: Commentary on stancetaking in motion', *Text & Talk*, 43(5), pp. 721–731.

Esposito, R. (2008) *Bios: Biopolitics and philosophy.* Translated by T. Campbell. Minneapolis: University of Minnesota Press.

Fausto-Sterling, A. (2000) *Sexing the body: Gender politics and the construction of sexuality.* New York: Basic Books.

Fausto-Sterling, A. (2005) 'The bare bones of sex: Part 1 – sex and gender', *Signs*, 30(2), pp. 1491–1527.

Fausto-Sterling, A. (2008) 'The bare bones of race', *Social Studies of Science*, 38(5), pp. 657–694.

Fausto-Sterling, A. (2012) *Sex/gender: Biology in a social world*. London: Routledge.

Feder, E. K. (2009) 'Imperatives of normality: From "intersex" to "disorders of sex development"', *GLQ: A Journal of Lesbian and Gay Studies*, 15(2), pp. 225–247.

Feder, E. K. (2014) *Making sense of intersex: Changing ethical perspectives in biomedicine*. Indianapolis: Indiana University Press.

Foucault, M. (1978) *The history of sexuality, Volume 1: An introduction*. Translated by R. Hurley. New York: Vintage.

Foucault, M. (1980). *Herculine Barbin: Being the recently discovered memoirs of a nineteenth-century French hermaphrodite*. Translated by Richard McDougall. Brighton: Harvester Press.

Foucault, M. (1996) *Foucault live: Collected interviews, 1961–1984*. Edited by S. Lotringer. Translated by L. Hochroth and J. Johnston. New York: Semiotext(e).

Foucault, M. (2003) *'Society must be defended': Lectures at the Collège de France 1975–1976*. Edited by M. Bertani and A. Fontana. Translated by D. Macey. New York: Picador.

Gal, S. (2021) 'Gender and the discursive authority of far-right politics', *Gender & Language*, 15(1), pp. 96–103.

Giroux, H. A. (2008) 'Beyond the biopolitics of disposability: Rethinking neoliberalism in the New Gilded Age', *Social Identities*, 14(5), pp. 587–620.

Goffman, E. (1981) 'Footing', in E. Goffman (ed.) *Forms of talk*. Philadelphia: University of Pennsylvania Press, pp. 124–159.

Griffiths, D. A. (2018) 'Shifting syndromes: Sex chromosome variations and intersex classifications', *Social Studies of Science*, 48(1), pp. 125–148.

Grosz, E. (2004) *The nick of time: Politics, evolution and the untimely*. London: Routledge.

Guerrero-Fernández, J., González-Peramato, P., Estévez, A.R. *et al.* (2022) 'Consensus guide on prophylactic gonadectomy in different sex development', *Endocrinología, Diabetes y Nutrición*, 69(8), pp. 629–645.

Gumperz, J. J. (1999) 'On interactional sociolinguistic method', in C. Roberts and S. Sarangi (eds) *Talk, work and institutional order: Discourse in medical, mediation and management settings*. Berlin: De Gruyter Mouton, pp. 453–471.

Gumperz, J. J. (2015) 'Interactional sociolinguistics: A personal perspective', in D. Tannen, H. E. Hamilton and D. Schiffrin (eds) *The handbook of discourse analysis*. 2nd ed. New York: John Wiley & Sons, pp. 309–323.

Hegarty, P. and Lundberg, T. (2020) 'Beyond choosing umbrella terms: Two psychologists make sense of "intersex" for gender and sexuality studies scholars', in D. Feldmann, A. Keilhauer and R. Liebold (eds) *Zuordnungen in bewegung: Geschlecht und sexuelle orientierung quer durch die disziplinen*. Erlangen: FAU University Press, pp. 197–217.

Hegarty, P., Prandelli, M., Lundberg, T. *et al.* (2021) 'Drawing the line between essential and nonessential interventions on intersex characteristics with European health care professionals', *Review of General Psychology*, 25(1), pp. 101–114.

Hess, D. J. (2015) 'Undone science and social movements: A review and typology', in M. Gross and L. McGoey (eds) *The Routledge international handbook of ignorance studies*. Abingdon: Routledge, pp. 141–154.

Ho, A. (2008) 'The individualist model of autonomy and the challenge of disability', *Journal of Bioethical Inquiry*, 5(2–3), pp. 193–207.

Ho, C., Earp, B.D., Kraus, C., Carpenter, M. and Wilkinson, D.J.C. (2025) 'Malignancy risk in Turner Syndrome+Y, early gonadectomy, and the ethics of parental choices', *Pediatrics*, 156(2), pp. 59–65.

Holmes, M. (2008) 'Mind the gaps: Intersex and (re-productive) spaces in disability studies and bioethics', *Journal of Bioethical Inquiry*, 5(2–3), pp. 169–181.

Holmes, M. (2009) 'Introduction: Straddling past, present, and future', in M. Holmes (ed.) *Critical intersex*. Farnham: Ashgate, pp. 1–12.

Holmes, M. (2011) 'The intersex enchiridion: Naming and knowledge', *Somatechnics*, 1(2), pp. 388–411.

Huang, Y.-P., Huang, Y.P., Wang, S.Y, Kellett, U. and Chen, C.H. (2020) 'Shame, suffering, and believing in the family: The experiences of grandmothers of a grandchild with a developmental delay or disability in the context of Chinese culture', *Journal of Family Nursing*, 26(1), pp. 52–64.

Hughes, I. A., Houk, C., Ahmed, S.F. *et al.* (2006) 'Consensus statement on the management of intersex disorders', *Archives of Disease in Childhood*, 91(7), pp. 554–563.

Hutton, C. (2019) *The tyranny of ordinary meaning: Corbett v Corbett and the invention of legal sex*. Cham: Palgrave Macmillan.

Inckle, K. (2015) 'Debilitating times: Compulsory ablebodiedness and white privilege in theory and practice', *Feminist Review*, 111(1), pp. 42–58.

Jablonka, E. and Lamb, M. J. 2005. *Evolution in four dimensions: Genetic, epigenetic, behavioural, and symbolic variation in the history of life.* Cambridge, MA: The MIT Press.

Jaworski, A. and Thurlow, C. (2009) 'Taking an elitist stance: Ideology and the discursive production of social distinction', in A. Jaffe (ed.) *Stance: Sociolinguistic perspectives.* Oxford: Oxford University Press, pp. 195–226.

Jenkins, T. M. and Short, S. E. (2017) 'Negotiating intersex: A case for revising the theory of social diagnosis', *Social Science & Medicine*, 175, pp. 91–98.

Jones, T. (2017) 'Intersex and families: Supporting family members with intersex variations', *Journal of Family Strengths*, 17(2), pp. 1–29.

Jordan-Young, R. M. (2010) *Brain Storm: The flaws in the science of sex differences.* Cambridge, MA: Harvard University Press.

Jordan-Young, R. M. and Karkazis, K. (2019) *Testosterone: An unauthorized biography.* Cambridge, MA: Harvard University Press.

Karhu, S. (2022) 'Gender skepticism, trans livability, and feminist critique', *Signs*, 47(2), pp. 295–317.

Karkazis, K. (2008) *Fixing sex: Intersex, medical authority, and lived experience.* Durham: Duke University Press.

Karkazis, K. (2019) 'The misuses of "biological sex"', *The Lancet*, 394(10212), pp. 1898–1899.

Kessler, S. J. (1990) 'The medical construction of gender: Case management of intersexed infants', *Signs*, 16(1), pp. 3–26.

Kiesling, S. F. (2009) 'Style as stance: Stance as the explanation for patterns in sociolinguistic variation', in A. Jaffe (ed.) *Stance: Sociolinguistic perspectives.* Oxford: Oxford University Press, pp. 171–194.

Kiesling, S. F. (2018) 'Masculine stances and the linguistics of affect: On masculine ease', *NORMA: International Journal for Masculinity Studies*, 13(3–4), pp. 191–212.

Kiesling, S. F. (2020) 'Investment in a model of stancetaking: I mean and just sayin'', *Language Sciences*, 82, pp. 1–20.

Kiesling, S. F. (2022) 'Stance and stancetaking', *Annual Review of Linguistics*, 8(1), pp. 410–426.

King, B. W. (2022a) 'Biopolitics and intersex human rights: A role for applied linguistics', in C. W. Chun (ed.) *Applied linguistics and politics.* London: Bloomsbury, pp. 155–181.

King, B. W. (2022b) 'Epilogue: Geopolitical lenses (and mirrors) in workplace language and gender research', in L. Mullany and S. Schnurr (eds) *Globalisation, geopolitics, and gender in professional Communication.* Abingdon: Routledge, pp. 213–223.

King, B. W. (2023a) 'Beyond undoing raciolinguistics – Biopolitics and the concealed confluence of sociolinguistic perspectives', *Journal of Sociolinguistics*, 27(5), pp. 436–440.

King, B. W. (2023b) 'Communicating health knowledges across clinic and community', in O. Zayts-Spence and S. M. Bridges (eds) *Language, health and culture*. Abingdon: Routledge, pp. 101–118.

King, B. W. (forthcoming) 'Abnormal deceivers? Biopower in clinician accounts of embodiment and life for people with intersex variations' [peer review].

King, B. W., Dayrell, C. and Zorzi, V. (2026) 'Risk and danger on the rise: Representation of intersex variations of innate sex characteristics in biomedical research', *Social Science and Medicine* 389(118808), pp. 1–11.

Köhler, B., Kleinemeier, E., Lux, A. et al. (2012) 'Satisfaction with genital surgery and sexual life of adults with XY disorders of sex development: Results from the German Clinical Evaluation Study', *The Journal of Clinical Endocrinology & Metabolism*, 97(2), pp. 577–588.

Koyama, E. and Weasel, L. (2002) 'From social construction to social justice: Transforming how we teach about intersexuality', *Women's Studies Quarterly*, 30(3/4), pp. 169–78.

Lara-Otero, K., Guerra, C., Cheng, J.K.Y. et al. (2019) 'Genetic counselor and healthcare interpreter perspectives on the role of interpreters in cancer genetic counselling', *Health Communication*, 34(13), pp. 1608–1618.

Latour, B. (2004) 'Why has critique run out of steam? From matters of fact to matters of concern', *Critical Inquiry*, 30(2), pp. 225–248.

Lau, D. H. (2002) 'Patient empowerment: A patient-centred approach to improve care', *Hong Kong Medical Journal*, 8(5), pp. 372–374.

Leap, W. L. (2012) 'Queer linguistics, sexuality, and discourse analysis', in J. P. Gee and M. Handford (eds) *The Routledge handbook of discourse analysis*. 1st Ed. Abingdon: Routledge, pp. 558–571.

Leap, W. L. (2015) 'Queer linguistics as critical discourse analysis', in D. Tannen, H. E. Hamilton and D. Schiffrin (eds) *The handbook of discourse analysis*. New York: John Wiley & Sons, pp. 661–680.

Leap, W. L. (2023) 'Queer linguistics and discourse analysis', in M. Handford and J. P. Gee (eds) *The Routledge handbook of discourse analysis*. 2nd Ed. Abingdon: Routledge, pp. 203–216.

Lee, P. A., Nordenström, A., Houk, C.P. et al. (2016) 'Global disorders of sex development update since 2006: Perceptions, approach and care', *Hormone Research in Paediatrics*, 85(3), pp. 158–180.

Lee, P.-H. (2023) 'Un(ac)countable no-bodies: The politics of ignorance in global health policymaking', *Critical Public Health*, 33(1), pp. 48–59.

Lemke, T. (2005) 'A zone of indistinction: A critique of Giorgio Agamben's concept of biopolitics', *Outlines*, 7(1), pp. 3–13.

Lempert, M. (2009) 'On "flip-flopping": Branded stancetaking in U.S. electoral politics', *Journal of Sociolinguistics*, 13(2), pp. 223–248.

Li, D. C. S. (2017) *Multilingual Hong Kong: Languages, literacies and identities*. Cham: Springer.

Liao, L. M. (2022) 'Western management of intersex and the myth of patient-centred care', in M. Walker (ed.) *Interdisciplinary and global perspectives on intersex*. Cham: Palgrave Macmillan, pp. 241–262.

Liao, L. M. and Baratz, A. (2023) 'Medicalization of intersex and resistance: A commentary on Conway', *International Journal of Impotence Research*, 35(1), pp. 51–55.

Liao, L. M., Hegarty, P., Creighton, S., Lundberg, T. and Roen, K. *et al.* (2019) 'Clitoral surgery on minors: An interview study with clinical experts of differences of sex development', *BMJ Open*, 9(e025821), pp. 1–7.

Linell, P. (2009) *Rethinking language, mind, and world dialogically: Interactional and contextual theories of human sense-making*. Charlotte, NC: Information Age.

Lo, S. (2021) 'Hong Kong in 2020: National Security Law and truncated autonomy', *Asian Survey*, 61(1), pp. 34–42.

Lorber, J. (2021) *The new gender paradox: Fragmentation and persistence of the binary*. New York: John Wiley & Sons.

Loveland, K. (2017) 'Feminism against neoliberalism: Theorizing biopolitics in Germany, 1978–1993', *Gender & History*, 29(1), pp. 67–86.

Lu, L. (2008) 'Culture, self, and subjective well-being: Cultural psychological and social change perspectives', *Psychologia*, 51(4), pp. 290–303.

Luke, A. (2013) 'Regrounding critical literacy: Representation, facts and reality', in M. R. Hawkins (ed.) *Framing language and literacies: Socially situated views and perspectives*. Abingdon: Routledge, pp. 136–148.

Lundberg, D. J. and Chen, J. A. (2024) 'Structural ableism in public health and healthcare: A definition and conceptual framework', *The Lancet Regional Health – Americas*, 30(100650), 1–8.

Lundberg, T., Hegarty, P. and Roen, K. (2018) 'Making sense of "intersex" and "DSD": How laypeople understand and use terminology', *Psychology & Sexuality*, 9(2), pp. 161–173.

Malatino, H. (2019) *Queer embodiment: Monstrosity, medical violence, and intersex experience*. Lincoln: University of Nebraska Press.

Malatino, H. (2021) 'The promise of repair: Trans rage and the limits of feminist coalition', *Signs*, 46(4), pp. 827–851.

Markowitz, S. (2001) 'Pelvic politics: Sexual dimorphism and racial difference', *Signs*, 26(2), pp. 389–414.

Mbembe, A. (2019) *Necropolitics*. Durham, NC: Duke University Press.

McElhinney, B. (2003) 'Theorizing gender in sociolinguistics and linguistic anthropology', in J. Holmes and M. Meyerhoff (eds) *The handbook of language and gender*. Oxford: Blackwell, pp. 21–42.

McRuer, R. (2006) *Crip theory: Cultural signs of queerness and disability*. New York: New York University Press.

McWhorter, L. (1999) *Bodies and pleasures: Foucault and the politics of sexual normalization*. Bloomington: Indiana University Press.

McWhorter, L. (2009) *Racism and sexual oppression in Anglo-America: A genealogy*. Bloomington: Indiana University Press.

McWhorter, L. (2010) 'Darwin's invisible hand: Feminism, reprogenetics, and Foucault's analysis of neoliberalism', *The Southern Journal of Philosophy*, 48(Spindel Supplement), pp. 43–63.

Meyers, Q. (2022) 'Strange tensions: Legacies of the colonial racial history of trans identities and intersex subjectivities', *Transgender Studies Quarterly*, 9(2), pp. 199–210.

Milani, T. M. (2014) 'Queering masculinities', in S. Ehrlich, M. Meyerhoff and J. Holmes (eds) *The handbook of language, gender and sexuality*. 2nd Ed. Malden, MA: Wiley, pp. 260–278.

Milani, T. M. (2018) 'Queer performativity', in R. Barrett and K. Hall (eds) *The Oxford handbook of language and sexuality*. Online ed., 10 July. Oxford: Oxford University Press, pp. 1–22.

Mills, C. (2018) *Biopolitics*. Abingdon: Routledge.

Mills, S. and Mullany, L. (2011) *Language, gender and feminism: Theory, methodology and practice*. Abingdon: Routledge.

Mishler, E. G. (1984) *The Discourse of medicine: The dialectics of medical interviews*. Norwood, NJ: Ablex.

Mohr, S. (2019) 'Editorial: The biopolitics of masculinity (studies)', *NORMA: International Journal for Masculinity Studies*, 14(4), pp. 199–205.

Monro, S., Carpenter, M., Crocetti, D. *et al.* (2021) 'Intersex: Cultural and social perspectives', *Culture, Health & Sexuality*, 23(4), pp. 431–440.

Monro, S., Berry, A., Carpenter, M., Crocetti, D. and Wall, S.S. (2025) *Intersex, variations of sex characteristics, DSD: Critical approaches*. Abingdon: Routledge.

Morland, I. (2015) 'Gender, genitals, and the meaning of being human', in L. Downing, I. Morland and N. Sullivan (eds) *Fuckology: Critical essays on John Money's diagnostic concepts*. Chicago: University of Chicago Press, pp. 69–98.

Muschialli, L., Connor, L.A., Boy-Mena, E. et al. (2024) 'Perspectives on conducting "sex-normalizing" intersex surgeries conducted in infancy: A systematic review', *PLOS Global Public Health*, 4(8), p. e0003568.

Nyström, S. (2016) 'Names and meaning', in C. Hough and D. Izdebska (eds) *The Oxford handbook of names and naming*. Oxford: Oxford University Press, pp. 39–51.

Oakley, A. (1972) *Sex, gender and society*. London: Temple Smith.

Opel, D. J. (2017) 'A push for progress with shared decision-making in pediatrics', *Pediatrics*, 139(2), pp. 7–9.

Orr, C. E. (2023) *Cripping intersex*. Vancouver: University of British Columbia Press.

Oudshoorn, N. (1990) 'On the making of sex hormones: Research materials and the production of knowledge', *Social Studies of Science*, 20(1), pp. 5–33.

Pasterski, V., Prentice, P. and Hughes, I. A. (2010) 'Impact of the consensus statement and the new DSD classification system', *Best Practice & Research Clinical Endocrinology & Metabolism*, 24(1), pp. 187–195.

Pennycook, A. (2022) 'Critical applied linguistics in the 2020s', *Critical Inquiry in Language Studies*, 19(1), pp. 1–21.

Phyak, P. and Sah, P. K. (2024) 'Epistemic injustice and neoliberal imaginations in English as a medium of instruction (EMI) policy', *Applied Linguistics Review*, 15(4), pp. 1321–1343.

Pilnick, A. (2022) *Reconsidering patient centred care: Between autonomy and abandonment*. Bingley: Emerald.

Pilnick, A. (2023) 'Reconsidering patient-centred care: Authority, expertise and abandonment', *Health Expectations*, 26(5), pp. 1785–1788.

Pilnick, A. and Zayts, O. (2014) '"It's just a likelihood": Uncertainty as topic and resource in conveying "positive" results in an antenatal screening clinic', *Symbolic Interaction*, 37(2), pp. 187–208.

Prandelli, M. and Testoni, I. (2021) 'Inside the doctor's office: Talking about intersex with Italian health professionals', *Culture, Health & Sexuality*, 23(4), pp. 484–499.

Puar, J. K. (2017) *The right to maim: Debility, capacity, disability*. Durham: Duke University Press.

Rampton, B. (2016) 'Foucault, Gumperz and governmentality: Interaction, power and subjectivity in the twenty-first century', in J. Coupland (ed.) *Sociolinguistics: Theoretical debates*. Cambridge: Cambridge University Press, pp. 303–328.

Rathert, C., Wyrwich, M. D. and Boren, S. A. (2013). Patient-centered care and outcomes: A systematic review of the literature. *Medical Care Research and Review*, 70(4), pp. 351–379.

Reis, E. (2009) *Bodies in doubt: An American history of intersex*. Baltimore, MD: Johns Hopkins University Press.

Repo, J. (2014) Herculine Barbin and the omission of biopolitics from Judith Butler's gender genealogy. *Feminist Theory* 15(1), pp. 73–88.

Repo, J. (2016) *The biopolitics of gender*. Oxford: Oxford University Press.

Richardson, S. S. (2013) *Sex itself: The search for male and female in the human genome*. Chicago: Chicago University Press.

Roen, K. (2019) 'Intersex or diverse sex development: Critical review of psychosocial health care research and indications for practice', *The Journal of Sex Research*, 56(4–5), pp. 511–528.

Roen, K. (2023) 'Hypospadias surgery: Understanding parental emotions, decisions and regrets', *International Journal of Impotence Research*, 35(1), pp. 67–71.

Roen, K. and Hegarty, P. (2018) 'Shaping parents, shaping penises: How medical teams frame parents' decisions in response to hypospadias', *British Journal of Health Psychology*, 23(4), pp. 967–981.

Roen, K., Lundberg, T., Hegarty, P. and Liao, L.M. (2023) 'Whose responsibility is it to talk with children and young people about intersex/differences in sex development? Young people's, caregivers' and health professionals' perspectives', *Frontiers in Urology*, 3(1089198), pp. 1–12.

Rosa, J. and Flores, N. (2023) 'Undoing raciolinguistics, unsettling (socio)linguistics', *Journal of Sociolinguistics*, 27(5), pp. 483–485.

Rosario, V. A. (2009) 'Quantum sex: Intersex and the molecular deconstruction of sex', *GLQ: A Journal of Lesbian and Gay Studies*, 15(2), pp. 267–284.

Rowlett, B. J. L. and King, B. W. (2023) 'Merging mobilities: Querying knowledges, actions, and chronotopes in discourses of transcultural relationships from a North/South queer contact zone', *Critical Discourse Studies*, 20(2), pp. 111–127.

Rubin, D. A. (2016) 'Biochemistry and physiology', in N. A. Naples (ed.) *The Wiley Blackwell encyclopedia of gender and sexuality studies*. New York: John Wiley & Sons, pp. 1–7.

Rubin, D. A. (2017) *Intersex matters: Biomedical embodiment, gender regulation, and transnational activism*. Albany, NY: SUNY Press.

Rubin, D. A. (2021) 'Anger, aggression, attitude: Intersex rage as biopolitical protest', *Signs*, 46(4), pp. 987–1011.

Rubin, D. A. (2022) 'Intersex care', *Feminist Formations*, 34(2), pp. 178–187.

Russell, E. L. (2023) 'Linguistic engagement as public health: Anti-genderism and critical language scholarship for the twenty-first century', *Gender & Language*, 17(1), pp. 111–123.

Sanz, V. (2017) 'No way out of the binary: A critical history of the scientific production of sex', *Signs*, 43(1), pp. 2–27.

Scarry, E. (2011) *Thinking in an emergency*. New York: W.W. Norton.

Schiffrin, D. (1987) *Discourse markers*. Cambridge: Cambridge University Press.

Scott, J. W. (1996) *Only paradoxes to offer: French feminists and the rights of man*. Cambridge, MA: Harvard University Press.

Silva, D. N. and Borba, R. (2024) 'Sociolinguistics of hope: Language between the no-more and the not-yet', *Language in Society*, 53(5), pp. 775–790.

Siouta, E. and Olsson, U. (2020) 'Patient Centeredness from a perspective of history of the present: A genealogical analysis', *Global Qualitative Nursing Research*, 7(1), pp. 1–10.

So, A. Y. and Kwok, R.Y.-W., So, A.Y. (1995) 'Socioeconomic center, political periphery: Hong Kong's uncertain transition toward the twenty-first century', in *The Hong Kong-Guangdong link: Partnership in flux*. New York: Routledge, pp. 251–257.

Stivers, T. (2002). 'Participating in decisions about treatment: Overt parent pressure for antibiotic medication in pediatric encounters', *Social Science and Medicine*, 54(7), pp. 1111–1130.

Stryker, S. (2014) 'Biopolitics', *Transgender Studies Quarterly*, 1(1–2), pp. 38–41.

Stubbe, M., Dew, K., Macdonald, L. and Hunt, D. (2021) 'Interactional sociolinguistics: Tracking patient-initiated questions across an episode of care', in G. Brookes and D. Hunt (eds) *Analysing health communication: Discourse approaches*. Cham: Palgrave MacMillan, pp. 49–80.

Sullivan, N. (2015) 'The matter of gender', in L. Downing, I. Morland and N. Sullivan (eds) *Fuckology: Critical essays on John Money's diagnostic concepts*. Chicago: University of Chicago Press, pp. 19–40.

Swarr, A. L. (2023) *Envisioning African intersex: Challenging colonial and racist legacies in South African medicine*. Durham, NC: Duke University Press.

Tack, L. J. W. *et al*. (2019) 'Management of gonads in adults with androgen insensitivity: An international survey', *Hormone Research in Paediatrics*, 90(4), pp. 236–246.

Timmermans, S. *et al*. (2018) 'Does patient-centred care change genital surgery decisions? The strategic use of clinical uncertainty in disorders of sex development clinics', *Journal of Health and Social Behavior*, 59(4), pp. 520–535.

Timmermans, S. *et al.* (2019) 'Gender destinies: Assigning gender in Disorders of Sex Development-Intersex clinics', *Sociology of Health & Illness*, 41(8), pp. 1520–1534.

Tremain, S. L. (2017) *Foucault and feminist philosophy of disability*. Ann Arbor: University of Michigan Press.

Tuana, N. (2004) 'Coming to understand: Orgasm and the epistemology of ignorance', *Hypatia*, 19(1), pp. 194–232.

Tuana, N. (2006) 'The speculum of ignorance: The women's health movement and epistemologies of ignorance', *Hypatia*, 21(1), pp. 1–19.

Ussher, J. M. *et al.* (2024) '"I've had constant fears that I'll get cancer": The construction and experience of medical intervention on intersex bodies to reduce cancer risk', *International Journal of Qualitative Studies on Health and Well-Being*, 19(1), pp. 1–19.

Wetherell, M. (2012). *Affect and emotion: A new social science understanding*. Thousand Oaks, CA: Sage.

Wolff, M., Rubin, D. A. and Swarr, A. L. (2022) 'The intersex issue: An introduction', *Transgender Studies Quarterly*, 9(2), pp. 143–159.

Yeung, S. and Gray, J. (2023) 'Neoliberalism, English, and spoiled identity: The case of a high-achieving university graduate in Hong Kong', *Language in Society*, 52(4), pp. 595–616.

Zayts-Spence, O., Fung, J. L. F. and Chung, B. H. Y. (2021) '"Do language and culture really matter?": A trans-disciplinary investigation of cultural diversity in genetic counseling in Hong Kong', *Journal of Genetic Counselling*, 30(1), pp. 75–84.

Zeiler, K. and Wickström, A. (2009) 'Why do "we" perform surgery in newborn intersexed children? The phenomenology of the parental experience of having a child with intersex anatomies', *Feminist Theory*, 10(3), pp. 359–377.

Zimman, L. (2021) 'Beyond the cis gays' cis gaze: The need for a trans linguistics', *Gender & Language*, 15(3), pp. 423–429.

Zottola, A. and Borba, R. (2022) '"Gender ideology" and the discursive infrastructure of a transnational conspiracy theory', in M. Demata, V. Zorzi and A. Zottola (eds) *Conspiracy theory discourses*. Amsterdam: John Benjamins, 465–488.

Acknowledgments

I acknowledge funding from the Hong Kong Research Grants Council (GRF Project Number: 17621819), HKU Faculty of Arts (Start-up Research Grant), and the Mainland Affairs Office of Hong Kong (Sino-British Fellowship Trust Visitorship).

I would like to thank Peter Hegarty, Benedict Rowlett, Helen Sauntson, and Jaspal Naveel Singh for providing invaluable critical readings of earlier drafts. Thank you also to Meredith Marra and Paul Baker for hosting me at your institutions during critical writing phases. Sincere thanks also to two reviewers who provided valuable feedback.

Cambridge Elements =

Language, Gender and Sexuality

Helen Sauntson
York St John University

Helen Sauntson is Professor of English Language and Linguistics at York St John University, UK. Her research areas are language in education and language, gender and sexuality. She is co-editor of *The Palgrave Studies in Language, Gender and Sexuality* book series, and she sits on the editorial boards of the journals *Gender and Language* and the *Journal of Language and Sexuality*. Within her institution, Helen is Director of the Centre for Language and Social Justice Research.

Editorial Board
Lilian Lem Atanga, *The University of Bamenda*
Eva Nossem, *Saarland University*
Joshua M. Paiz, *The George Washington University*
M. Agnes Kang, *University of Hong Kong*

About the Series
Cambridge Elements in Language, Gender and Sexuality highlights the role of language in understanding issues, identities and relationships in relation to multiple genders and sexualities. The series provides a comprehensive home for key topics in the field which readers can consult for up-to-date coverage and the latest developments.

Cambridge Elements

Language, Gender and Sexuality

Elements in the Series

The Language of Gender-Based Separatism
Veronika Koller, Alexandra Krendel and Jessica Aiston

Queering Sexual Health Translation Pedagogy
Piero Toto

Legal Categorization of 'Transgender': An Analysis of Statutory Interpretation of 'Sex', 'Man', and 'Woman' in Transgender Jurisprudence
Kimberly Tao

LGBTQ+ and Feminist Digital Activism: A Linguistic Perspective
Angela Zottola

Feminism, Corpus-assisted Research and Language Inclusivity
Federica Formato

Queering Language Revitalisation: Navigating Identity and Inclusion among Queer Speakers of Minority Languages
John Walsh, Michael Hornsby, Eva J. Daussà, Renée Pera-Ros, Samuel Parker, Jonathan Morris and Holly R. Cashman

Pride in Asia: Negotiating Ideologies, Localness, and Alternative Futures
Benedict J. L. Rowlett, Pavadee Saisuwan, Christian Go,
Li-Chi Chen and Mie Hiramoto

Language, Gender and Pregnancy Loss
Beth Malory

Discourse and Queer Sinophone Male Identities: A Western Immigrant Perspective
Phil Freestone

Linguistic Representations of Women in Old English Prose: A Corpus-Based Phraseological Study
Anna Cichosz and Tomasz Dobrogoszcz

Gender and Uptalk in Hong Kong English
Wilkinson Daniel Wong Gonzales, Chan Pui Yu Ivy, Zhang Xiaohan Harry, Ng Chui Yin Judy and Chung Yan Ching Karina

Language, Gender and Biopolitics: Meaning-Making and Intersex Variations in Healthcare
Brian W. King

A full series listing is available at: www.cambridge.org/ELGS

For EU product safety concerns, contact us at Calle de José Abascal, 56–1°,
28003 Madrid, Spain or eugpsr@cambridge.org.

www.ingramcontent.com/pod-product-compliance
Lightning Source LLC
LaVergne TN
LVHW011853060526
838200LV00054B/4306